OTHER BOOKS BY CLAYTON ESHLEMAN

—Poetry—

Mexico & North (1962)
Indiana (1969)
Altars (1971)
Coils (1973)
The Gull Wall (1975)
What She Means (1978)
Nights We Put the Rock Together (1980)
Hades in Manganese (1981)
Fracture (1983)
The Name Encanyoned River: Selected Poems 1960–1985 (1986)
Hotel Cro-Magnon (1989)

—Prose—

Antiphonal Swing: Selected Prose 1960–1985 (1989)
Novices: A Study of Poetic Apprenticeship (1989)

—Translations—

Pablo Neruda, Residence on Earth (1962)
César Vallejo, The Complete Posthumous Poetry (with José Rubia Barcia) (1978)
Antonin Artaud, Four Texts (with Norman Glass) (1982)
Aimé Césaire, The Collected Poetry (with Annette Smith) (1983)
Michel Deguy, Given Giving (1984)
Bernard Bador, Sea Urchin Harakiri (1986)
Conductors of the Pit: Major Works by Rimbaud, Vallejo, Césaire,
Artaud and Holan (1988)
Aimé Césaire, Lyric & Narrative Poetry 1946–1982 (with Annette Smith)
(1990)
César Vallejo, Trilce (1992)

—Editor—

Folio (Bloomington, Indiana, 3 issues, 1959–1960)
Quena (Lima, Peru, 1 issue, published & suppressed by
the North American Peruvian Cultural Institute, 1966)
Caterpillar (NYC–Los Angeles, 20 issues, 1967–1973)
A Caterpillar Anthology (material from issues #1–12, Doubleday, NYC, 1971)
Sulfur (Pasadena–Los Angeles–Ypsilanti, 34 issues, 1981–   )

Clayton ESHLEMAN

Under WORLD ARREST

SANTA ROSA *Black Sparrow Press* 1994

ACKNOWLEDGMENTS

Many of these poems, often in much different versions, appeared in the following magazines: *Agni, The Alternative Press, American Letters & Commentary, Bouillabaisse, BullHead, Cellar Roots, Denver Quarterly, Drunken Boat, Electric Rexroth, Exquisite Corpse, Fag Rag, First Intensity, First Offense, Grand Street, House Organ, Intent, The Kenyon Review, Lift, Momentum, New American Writing, North Dakota Quarterly, Notus, origin, The Paris Review, Poetry Flash, River Styx, Split City, Sulfur, Talisman, Talus, Temblor, :that:, World Letter,* and *Wray.* "Picked up the Rotted Doormat" first appeared as a *Ta'Wil Broadside;* "Mortified Citizen" first appeared in *After the Storm: Poems on the Persian Gulf War* (Maisonneuve Press); "Out of the Kat Godeu" first appeared in *Joy! Praise! Jerome Rothenberg at 60* (Ta'Wil Books & Documents); "Epilogue" appeared as "At the Locks of Infinity" in *American Poets Say Goodbye to the 20th Century* (Four Walls Eight Windows). I thank Eastern Michigan University for a Sabbatical Leave, Fall 1992, which helped me in the completion of this manuscript.

Black Sparrow Press books are printed on acid-free paper.

LIBRARY OF CONGRESS CATALOGING-IN-PUBLICATION DATA

Eshleman, Clayton, 1935-
    Under world arrest / Clayton Eshleman.
        p.   cm.
    ISBN 0-87685-936-8 (cloth trade) : $25.00. — ISBN 0-87685-937-6 (signed cloth) : $30.00. — ISBN 0-87685-935-X (pbk.) : $13.00
    I. Title.
PS3555.S5U53   1994
813'.54—dc20
                                                                    94-16085
                                                                    CIP

OTHER BOOKS BY CLAYTON ESHLEMAN

—Poetry—

Mexico & North (1962)
Indiana (1969)
Altars (1971)
Coils (1973)
The Gull Wall (1975)
What She Means (1978)
Nights We Put the Rock Together (1980)
Hades in Manganese (1981)
Fracture (1983)
The Name Encanyoned River: Selected Poems 1960–1985 (1986)
Hotel Cro-Magnon (1989)

—Prose—

Antiphonal Swing: Selected Prose 1960–1985 (1989)
Novices: A Study of Poetic Apprenticeship (1989)

—Translations—

Pablo Neruda, Residence on Earth (1962)
César Vallejo, The Complete Posthumous Poetry (with José Rubia Barcia) (1978)
Antonin Artaud, Four Texts (with Norman Glass) (1982)
Aimé Césaire, The Collected Poetry (with Annette Smith) (1983)
Michel Deguy, Given Giving (1984)
Bernard Bador, Sea Urchin Harakiri (1986)
Conductors of the Pit: Major Works by Rimbaud, Vallejo, Césaire, Artaud and Holan (1988)
Aimé Césaire, Lyric & Narrative Poetry 1946–1982 (with Annette Smith) (1990)
César Vallejo, Trilce (1992)

—Editor—

Folio (Bloomington, Indiana, 3 issues, 1959–1960)
Quena (Lima, Peru, 1 issue, published & suppressed by the North American Peruvian Cultural Institute, 1966)
Caterpillar (NYC–Los Angeles, 20 issues, 1967–1973)
A Caterpillar Anthology (material from issues #1–12, Doubleday, NYC, 1971)
Sulfur (Pasadena–Los Angeles–Ypsilanti, 34 issues, 1981–   )

Clayton ESHLEMAN

Under WORLD ARREST

SANTA ROSA *Black Sparrow Press* 1994

ACKNOWLEDGMENTS

Many of these poems, often in much different versions, appeared in the following magazines: *Agni, The Alternative Press, American Letters & Commentary, Bouillabaisse, BullHead, Cellar Roots, Denver Quarterly, Drunken Boat, Electric Rexroth, Exquisite Corpse, Fag Rag, First Intensity, First Offense, Grand Street, House Organ, Intent, The Kenyon Review, Lift, Momentum, New American Writing, North Dakota Quarterly, Notus, origin, The Paris Review, Poetry Flash, River Styx, Split City, Sulfur, Talisman, Talus, Temblor, :that:, World Letter,* and *Wray.* "Picked up the Rotted Doormat" first appeared as a *Ta'Wil* Broadside; "Mortified Citizen" first appeared in *After the Storm: Poems on the Persian Gulf War* (Maisonneuve Press); "Out of the Kat Godeu" first appeared in *Joy! Praise! Jerome Rothenberg at 60* (Ta'Wil Books & Documents); "Epilogue" appeared as "At the Locks of Infinity" in *American Poets Say Goodbye to the 20th Century* (Four Walls Eight Windows). I thank Eastern Michigan University for a Sabbatical Leave, Fall 1992, which helped me in the completion of this manuscript.

Black Sparrow Press books are printed on acid-free paper.

LIBRARY OF CONGRESS CATALOGING-IN-PUBLICATION DATA

Eshleman, Clayton, 1935-
    Under world arrest / Clayton Eshleman.
        p.   cm.
    ISBN 0-87685-936-8 (cloth trade) : $25.00. — ISBN 0-87685-937-6 (signed cloth) :
$30.00. — ISBN 0-87685-935-X (pbk.) : $13.00
    I. Title.
PS3555.S5U53   1994
813'.54—dc20   94-16085
                                                                                    CIP

To two painters who,
facing power and cruelty,
have offered in return
a commanding vision of integrity and moral rigor,
to my old friends and comrades,
Leon Golub and Nancy Spero,

and to
the unnamed Salvadoran child
dug up at El Mozote,
where 1000 peasants were massacred,
"who died with a tiny pencil and a few coins in her pocket,"

I dedicate *Under*
World
Arrest.

CONTENTS

PREFACE

"Under World Arrest" was initially called "Abyss." By 1991, that title no longer seemed capable of concentrating the strands of the book into a single image. While the abyss, or gap between worlds, plays an active role in the book, its depth is intersected by other factors.

The earliest underworlds and the origin of image have been re-visioned in my poetry for years. However, having pushed back to the primal places of ensouling, as underworlds they appear to be in arrest. This does not mean that they are dead—it means that when I crouch in Combarelles, decorated at 13,000 BCE, and attempt to read the walls, there is most definitely an abyss between subject and object that, to my knowledge, may only be crossed in poetry.

I would hold my imagination accountable not only for a crossing of this abyss, but for what the historian Henry Steele Commager has identified as America's "unacknowledged, unrepented crimes," a documentation brought into the present by Noam Chomsky, Michael Parenti, Michael Kelly, and Mark Danner, among others. While I am open to the invention of "new worlds," I insist on inventing them while addressing the cruelty of the present one. Thus the title of this book is also modeled on the political incarceration known as "under house arrest." I place myself under world arrest and refuse to release myself from the complexities of an eros that while not cruel in itself is congruent to the news reports of the suffering of others and must make its way into articulation burdened by its awareness.

Whatever depth these poems have, whatever primary sources they may evoke, they attempt to press themselves to the surfaces and edges of present reality, to assimilate it in its full intensity. One must be under world arrest, for to my mind there is no exit, no escape from human peril here and now or ever.

> If this destiny is to have meaning, then this meaning must be born out of the heart of this very destiny and within its unsurpassable borders set by Necessity; it can only be revealed by my 'stewing' in whatever happens. Never could it lie in a subsequent event, in a future or a beyond. If each fateful event does not itself unfold its meaning, then there is no meaning at all.
>
> [Wolfgang Giegerich: *Deliverance from the Stream of Events: Okeanos and the Circulation of the Blood,* 1988]

[Ypsilanti,
January, 1994]

UNDER WORLD ARREST

SHORT STORY

Begin with this: the world has no origin.
We encircle the moment, lovers
who, encircling each other, steep in
                    the fantasy:
now we know the meaning of life.

Wordsworth's *recollection*: wreck election,
the coddling of ruins, as if the oldest man
                    thinking of the earliest thing
offers imagination its greatest bounty.

A poem is a snake sloughing off the momentary,
crawling out of now (the encasement of
                    its condition)
into layered, mattered, time.
Now is the tear and ear of terra's torn era.
For the serpentine, merely a writhe
                    in appetite.

We posit Origin in order to posit End,

and if your drinking water is sewage,
to do so is understandable.

When the water is pure, Lilith's anatomy
is glimpsable in each drop.

But the water is never pure.

Before time, there appears to have been
a glass of pure water.

Therefore, we speculate, after time,
there will be another.

Life, a halo surrounding emptiness.

Continue with this: not body vs. soul,
but the inherent doubleness of any situation.
Thus in fusion there is also abyss.

Conclusion: I am suspended between origin and now,
or between origin and a bit before now.
Unknotting myself from both ends,
I drop through the funnel the y in abyss offers.

Nothing satisfies. And,
my suffering is nothing. Two postage stamps
glued, back to back,
abysscadabra.

What is missing? A poetry so full of claws
as to tear the reader's face off.
Too much? Look what men do to women.
Why should art be less?

Poetry's horrible responsibility:
in language to be the world.

[for Don Byrd]

16

THE BASHO THRILL OF SETTING FORTH,
potential illumination, potential demise.

Dissolution now tied to millennium,
our end and the world's throw
shafts of Don't Look Forward into all leaving,
all returning, creating an undertow
resplendent with abyss.

As if each moment were a preboarding inspection,
a Maya disassembly line,
the X-ray screens in the gods' octopodal eyes.

THE LOSS OF ETERNITY—
its effect on the poetic line,
as if the past to the left and the future
to the right had kept,
before ocean became mortal,
the line taut.

The exploded non-sequitur line.
The one word line. Lines so chatty
(or so cold) reader heart is to cross
directly to that poet
bypassing the poem's interim host.

I look at my lines. Often,
when I am saying what I want to say,
the line looks wrong. It deposits
my energy in sand-like trails that back
down, hammock-wise, are weighted
as a chrysalis? or with a body
dead? or in self-embrace?

"Done wore the motherfucker out!"
—gospel according to Bird.

AT THE HEARTH OF ARGUMENT

Mother
    smell   the timbre of symphonies.

Against the multichambered heart of Bruckner,
Bud Powell, all chain and frankincense,
           reddens the keyboard.

I almost smelled her corpse entangled with Powell
and stuffed into the groinwork of the piano
where the elves and fairies are splinters.

4705,
where Powell is bandaged and wet from speech fast.
Now the lights are turned off forever. Powell
dead. My mother dead. A garage with a Salvadoran's
car. 4705.

What draws me to those men and women heavy with female
elements, who grit their teeth and menstruate in the filth of
the spirit, the line a cuttlefish, strong with no spine.

When blood meets fire in a toke of hashish, all tumblers lock
in analogy. The danger is to believe fire and blood have been
wedded.

Everything of equal interest, that is the end of imagination.

Give a cock to this one, a cunt to that one, and teach them
both to forgive.

Nothing you can say is good enough unless you are reborn in the act of saying it.

The color in a self-foiled mind comes from the blood of creators and lives to take revenge on creators for constantly appearing to be its cause.

This means that I once and for all cease to judge men by the cavern their hauntedness drives them into.

Yet I still hold in my refusal to allow anyone his point if an argument could be in store.

And what else is that argument but my own cosmological despair.

My cosmological desire to translate my fury into an argument so few, so very few, are willing to have with me.

And not say man is not a monster
but to allow the fury
in a warfare where I have him
choked in the lattice of my language
and There
feel my threadbare self
replacing him.

                              [Sherman Oaks, 1972]

STILL-LIFE, WITH HUIDOBRO

Two guinea hen legs, an artichoke bottom, in an earthen bowl.

My partially-consumed parents, my partially-consumed self, not of them. Not of *their bird*. How so? Their breasts gone, their wings, I am picked clean of leaves,

I am heart tufted with choke.

Do we pull childhood through adolescence and reconstruct it as formal fantasy, as "organiz'd innocence," so that the poem is always in some sense *back there*—

or might a more severe transformation occur?

If mother is made imagination, I am no longer *her* child. She has been brought forward as: *invent new worlds*. The father then becomes: *and back up what you say*. A responsible avant-garde. When Blake rejects the rational, he sets up a lifelong struggle with the father.

Huidobro's "Inventa mundos nuevos y cuida tu palabra" contains the contraries in which a poetry might live. At one extreme, the poem is nearly fantasy—at the other, nearly observation. In each extreme, yin-yang-wise, a pulse of the other asserts, the rhythm reverses.

Vision is not prior to reality, but reality is vision's material.

[Les Bois d'Envaux]

OUTTAKES

He wanted the synthesis *and* the mêlée,
wanted to eat himself, be utterly outside himself,
    to keep on perishing.
Wanted the kinks in the muss, the stuff stuck to
    the brush,
what clings to the elevator in the drain,
the spit-out toothpaste, all the rejected passengers
    plus their progeny.
He wanted to be the equatorial line stammering with
    the input of warring opposites.

Merely for the sensation of being above himself,
    unlike a spider,
he looked down upon himself, was his own web.
Whistling down the firepole mother,
he jumped before the abyss and, like a dazed fly,
embraced the person with whom life was possible.
By doing so he abandoned the millions who wanted to pile
    in bed with him,
to bully him through the wall of paradise, to,
    by multiple fractures,
enspindle him with paradise.
But did he have the sense to love himself?
To respect what he disputed?
To dispute what he loved?
Because he was tactless, he was an asshole.
As an asshole, he was never praised.
This baffled him and made him better.
As better, he was spat upon
because he was not entirely tactless.

22

Taking it all into consideration,
trimming the fat, but adding it to the scales,
adding a pound for farts, jeers, disgusting remarks,
sleeping too late, putting on weight,
being out of a job, making the wrong face,
not shaving, not getting hard, getting hard too often,
being hard and not hard, forgetting her keys,
taking credit for everything, snoring—
taking it all into consideration,
add this to the far side of the beam:

    Anus-eyed Saturn, the
    tears frozen in his plumbing,

    loves to have his eyes put out
    by Dionysus's

    penile interrogations.
    Look at them, my soul,

    a couple of elderly
    infants, both pregnant with

    chains, coils of vines, laurel
    growing through the links.

    Study them, my soul, help
    them up onto the incubus

    delivery platform,
    and there ravish them!

    Relinquish the hold of
    "no ideas but in things."

THERE IS NEITHER FATHER NOR MOTHER
  when I am made.

My blood is created from the fruit
  of first forms.

Of elephant graveyards
Of pulled-out eternity staves
Of the sensation of orgasm as the goad
  of all one's power
Of the flowering of shrubbery
Of the earliest horned god carved of
  stalagmitic drippings
Of blue veins and vermilion glans
Of the last passenger pigeon
  burst in tar
Of the nipple at strut with the goose step
  of the cock
Of the face of Art Pepper
Of bruised American pie
Of what in each artist must be a match
  for the infinite

NEGATION'S MATE

One translates Artaud by wrapping a page of his writing about one's cock, by working the writing into one's cock, and in the massage working Artaud out as the language of one's sperm,
    which must infuriate the spectre of Artaud
    and make it crawl on the Anglo page, not as English, but as an American page, subtle semen, crawling across the floor with a message, for the reader, from Artaud,
    which is to propose that Artaud is in all men, as, say, Montaigne is not, as the semen-colored human-shaped force crawling out of the sea, out of the hells that make up
    the lower male body,
    its bayonets, flame-throwers, lynch knots, racks, its medieval gym of iron chairs, winches, and thumb-screws,
    to which must be added a collective witch howl, or the coalesced sound of nine million women,
    brain as one ball,
    testicle as the other,
    as the male is a rotating dumbbell male mind like a cheerleader twirls in the ever-returning inquisitional gym,
    except that: Artaud was a kind person, and probably struck no one, probably struck only himself, not with fists, but as a coin is struck, minted, as a medal. He struck a gong off himself, masturbating at Rodez over an inquisitional model of the earth, or the feces of bats, and mice, he added his own, topologically, which he then rained upon, repeating the creation of the earth.
    It is this crude, desperate, transgressional and blasphemous creation that one translates when one actually does translate Artaud,
    and the pearl-grey language, like an endless earthworm,

out at the wrong hour in spring, too encouraged by rain, now
feels the sun in its "rable," as they say of hare, in its meaty loin,
   and is as sad as the earthworms on the sidewalk
   through which we rabble step
   when we read Artaud.

   *

"Remain a virgin," Artaud said to Florence Loeb, sweeping
her in to the grape press beneath his greatcoat. It was Mont-
parnasse, 1947, and Florence has remained there, a purple sigil
in the air, to this very day
   (though she physically lives to the west of Paris, with a
kitchen amphitheater, a visiting Himalayan guru, and stacks
of *Van Gogh le suicidé de la société* in the upstairs guest room)
   (it is in the living room that one most keenly feels Artaud,
his head drawn by himself as if beheaded, with a coffee stain
across the empty root that passes for his neck . . .)

   *

Every male poet has a handful of daughters he works like metal
balls in his palm facing the interrogation of critics and en-
thusiasts,
   are these your children? their noses point at the pile of
scraps accumulated on his night stand,
   and so he works his steel balls, his daughter-loaded bobs,
guilty
   of not having so inseminated the world
   —"Press close, O bare-bosomed night!"—
that the abyss between intention and the thing itself closes,
seals, and in the sealing
   ignites his mutinous chorus . . .

   *

Every male poet carries a whore around in his pocket, she's
a kind of lighter for the compost he is constantly popping be-
tween his lips,

26

you know, the detritus upon which he draws, to inhale a bit of soul,

for ensouling is the primary process,

and it is ignited, or stoked, with censored scenes below censored scenes,

degradation too hideous to be observed by one who is not an actual torturer, the Serb, say, who raped the young mother on the floor by her newborn, then blew its brains out as she watched—

Calley married into the Vicks Jewelry Store family in Columbus, Georgia, and his hands begin to perspire still when people walk in and ask about My Lai

but sheer evil is a distraction, no?

Artaud and Miller work off whores,

who are not evil, but are pocked with the serpent-work of the upswept breath of men, the sausage odor of nostrils, the grime under fingernails, as the finger twists inside

what Somalis clitordictate.

My sympathy goes out to all those artists who, like garbage scows, move through the universe, at siphon, inducting into their weave the cruelty of others,

for wrath, evil, and the abomination of person, are not easy to digest.

What Has Been Left Out, always the book to be written.

AMPHIMIXIS

Deep in the body wilderness,
there is a curved, ornate bridge
linking fecundity and death,
the upper rim of the Muladhara Chakra,
our "root support."

On this bridge wrapped in moonlit fog,
by sacked Artaud, a woman crouches,
in lemon kimono, bald head bowed.

Your mother is not personal,
she has no face,
her body is serpentine,
her breasts are the double gates
at which your whole life
tugs.

INDIANA IN THE NIGHT SKY

Again! before the podium, the mass of yellow sheets
on which are written the poems I am to read—
mostly blank. What is under the work
                    is again showing through.
        To write is to scratch with a knife
on a boulder my body is stretched across.
I make an order at one point in the vast
                    skin of things
and now must hunt for what I am sure I had prepared.
In this repeated dream, last night
I finally found something I could read.
A murderer spoke, mostly grunts I mouthed
                    to audience satisfaction?

        the dream frayed . . . I half-awoke
intent upon seeing what correspondence there might be
between blankness erasing my words
and only being able to control the situation
                    as a murderer.
My mother was again present,
ill and dead, fixedly in bed,
needing constant attention.
Which illness would I attend?
Her room was hived with doors.
I locked the Oedipal one,
                    cutting back
to the living room where, in 1966,
reading *The Function of the Orgasm*,
    I confronted her.
"I don't love you like you think I do."

That night, I slipped down into my basement
    teen-age nook and wrote:

Today I have set my crowbar against all I know
In a shower of soot & blood
Breaking the backbone of my mother

Because she died 4 years later of spinal cancer
I have the fantasy that somehow
those written words, which I don't think she read,
    are embodied in
what I actually did say in the living room,
that I was fated to gain independence from her
                        and from Indiana
only by killing something there,
that I was to know the power of the word
via associating breaking my mother's backbone
    with the illness that killed her!

Now, I believe that this is not true—
but why is it trenchant?
Having to appear as a murderer
to be able to break the hold of the blank
                    or, erased, page.
I needed the negative aspect of my freedom
to confront the exultation of my absurdity.
The nothingness swarming these ordered lines
    scoops them up,
or comes up from below, as if the boulder
I scratch thoughts into
                    has the power to shrug,
effacing my remarks, restoring its mother purity.

MARGINALIA TO BAUDELAIRE

Do you recall, my soul,
the one who tormented you for years,
your first night with her,
like a small cat, curled in your arms,
while, in entering her,
you almost put her on! And upon waking—
her breath—a dead mouse!
A few moments, and she coiled again.
How easily you seduced yourself
to brave
the corpse
within
    her,
for years
what Krishna
gambled,
your dreams
displayed,
gamboling on
    Cobra
Bouquet!

THE SIXTIES

Comfort is rare wine.
It moves me today to think how
particular nodes of others'
words hang, beautiful dead moments
I can visit—
                Jim Tenney's words,
some 20 years ago: "Does she turn you on?"
"No." "Then you can't live with her."
He could have waited until I returned
to the house and then asked:
"What's wrong?" But he came down to the creek
50 yards from his house where I'd gone,
overcharged with LSD, to cry.

I then looked into my cry: sex and love were not
to be divided—better be alone
than re-drape that fence, at 12,
head over Jeannie Woodring's backyard grass,
ass facing my parent's bedroom.

So Jim and I walked, hand in hand,
home across New Paltz Road,
torrid July heat
the acid had stoked into Edenic roar,
like all Edens poised on the peristaltic
waves of a jeweled worm's back.

                *

Recalling the late night on Matilija 1970
dancing to "The Friends of Distinction" four of us
chimneyed, a four-square dancing,
the heat rising through the walls our bodies made . . .

What if what I felt then could be released into the world?
(Reich's vision of mobilizing the energy of a football
    stadium crowd in the service of mankind)
You Jim puking every morning on purpose
        to lift the orgasm through our chests
not to contain it no matter how many lotus petals for
            the mind

—or was I simply whipped against
the revolving walls of withheld orgy?

Down where our feet were shuffling:
hearth-blackened sweeps
like spider-thousands trying to climb out of hell

a Gestapo shaft

        the energy intoxication taps
braided on the mobile corral of our shoulders and arms.

                    [1986]

BROWN STUDY

Lying in bed, late at night, feeling her otherness.
I will never match it, assimilate it.
To prevent such feelings, men engage in conquest.
A new confidence is always starting up in Hell. Somewhere out there Jesse Helms has restrung the instruments and is now standing up on four back legs, dipping his chopsticks (or chopping his dipstick) into the lovers' dinner.
These hands pressed in prayer—are they not shark fins cutting the bedroom air?
Let your cheeks sag, your eyes moisten, be your mother, have your father in you.
Self is a dubious eraser glued to vanishing lead.
Now the hairline between being and blackout can be visited. In it, I see that sometimes I am not even a grasshopper on crutches, before a den of festive ants in spiked heels strutting through the spider orders, each with a hard-on bigger than each of my semen lagoons.
To remove otherness from the other.
To experience difference as equality.

DOUBLE PELICAN

I dip my spout into your sex. Your retort,
  where all things get retwisted,
magma-bubble-gulps my mind. Then we spin,
  a cross in orbit, Magdalenian.

The miracle is: simultaneously your spout
  penetrates my navel.
I feel your interest spread, like ganglia.
  Our missing story flows lawlessly.

We, the shadow of each,
  neither prior, nor dominant.

The gist is to grip the seamless jet of
  shadow squid, to be ludic
commandos slipping through the basis of
  mind. Embraced within you,

I see your centripetally-closed plates
  fan wide. My spout becomes
the flute of an empyramided king. I charm
  your cobra. You hood my sex.

Tentacles of human coherence.

QUOTIDIAN SPECTRES

November winds. Mammoths wheel and bay
     over librarial vaults.
Somehow archaic pride, somehow our unforgivable
promotion of slaughter in Salvador—
they do not balance. I want them twisting
on a single word stem, a stem with scale, vitally
     out, in turbulence with

earth in menstrual nomenclature and devourer
     monoculture,
the anti the ir the ism aliases—desire of all poets

to open *seshemu*, to penetrate paradise
and tell tales of the heart to the other until it dawns
Cairo or Leningrad, and the metaphor transfers,
     thou art.

          *

          Luxor Yaxchilan Lascaux
are you spectres or emanations?
The streets of NYC are as lice upon TV screens,
"news" through which we worship detergent.
     And the alley I walk today?
I marvel at its lack of sturdy borders, admire its cans,
house and auto rears, visible dirt under pebbles.
It is more "everyday" than impersonal American streets.
I walk a multi-level memory alley, a midden
     loaded with alley-walked moment.

          *

36

Today the Salvadoran Army is ripping open peasants
as I climb 6 flights to 100 *Sulfur* mss., *Trilce* in focus.
I want to force that Army to cross my footsteps here.
Why, fool, would you want to do that? Just to realize
                              a context?
The wish to die for a context, to be part of a text-tilling,
part of a surrounding magnanimity in which anima
      —but that too is a desurrounded word
          anima, without context,
      how might I wrap her in contextual pelt?

          *

Always, in our time, desire without a coordinate terminal.
Visits to Vladimir Holan, twice, stopped at the door,
his wife, tear-stained, only family invited in.
So we speak to Vladimir, in bed, via Mrs. Holan.
He sends out tiny, signed books—he is only 10 feet away!

Weight as a good seems to have departed.
The poem is fasting, unaware of why,
without touching down. To not touch down—
Postmodernism? My credentials are:
      have pit, will travel,

          will make love to the literal.
Not "screw" the literal, but caress
                the surface still-life,

elephant faces hacked off for a used flight-jacket,

famished Liberians scraping the docks with cardboard for
oil-trampled rice,

men shaking hands in a vat of spermaceti not on a whaling
ship but in the body of the other.

          *

37

A horse head. A horse-head-sized vulva
    superimposed across its neck.
The core of creativity is feminine—
but soul comes from the kill.

[Incised stone
block, Abri
Cellier.
28,000 BCE]

Nothing is absolutely dead?
Bakhtin's last words will not shield us
from the blizzard the mind must bear:
Russians at night, in zero cold,
standing in line to buy brick-like
    bars of ice-cream,
being unloaded from a crate.

[Leningrad,
1989]

THE POWER ROOM

The path along the rockface
unloads its spiritum as I pass.
              Out of cliff stain,
survival smoke tangles my head,
   raccoon human iguana stork layers,
          anima mundi face,
the human less than a quarter.

Like garter shreds, or pubic rust,
lichen dangles from the deep overhang.

Off a black gob on flagstone
a squad of flies lifts and holds in circus
   tent formation. Out of honey-
combed mouths the clowning dead roll in.
One could spend a lifetime
listening, as they attempt to tarantella
   back into organic light.

I took a whiff of Vézère papermill sewage
and dropped into the power room.
Rock pods through which vulvae emerged.
Vulva crossed horse neck, 6 cupules
       in search of a vulva.
Fertility-tallied, butt-gashed vulvae
or vulva-gashed buttocks or buttocks bagged
or buttocks plugged or body-slashed
vulvabutt, in stone atoned.
     A woman running into a wall

(Les Eyzies,
Regional Pre-
history Museum,
2nd floor,
incised stone
blocks,
28,000 BCE]

39

byabyssembraced. Cupule-jeweled phallus.
Peter Redgrove
perched on a head-shaped vulva-carved rock:

"I fell through the English mud
and kept on falling until I hit
this rock, whose molar-pouted mouth
utters a stripe of wild strawberries.
I am delighted in fallen
as well as in risen states,
and should Hades glue me here,
he can have my ass! I'll also leave my cock
like a bee-stinger in this vulva's brain,
flutter back to Falmouth
more spirally tone than man."

I was too embarrassed to publish what I saw in the Seine
when I was told James Wright had died,
but I told Redgrove now. I saw Wright's corpse
    in a moored barge—the Celan coffer?
belly-swarmed by Spicer and Crane,
avid for Wright's warm liver, like one tears out
    crab grass, or in Rashōmon's
crossbeam, the hag wrenched wig hair.

In imagination,
such exchange is never merely the father/son diathesis.
It is sheer hubris to sublimate otherness,
to emball it in our word web.
Poetry
is to let the other fall
into our nest, a rock
among our eggs, or
an egg among . . .
What glints are the ingot backs of snails,
fertilizing lore perhaps to be used,
whose curving walls are loaded
with the root history of our plasmic halo.

40

SOME COMMENTS BY THE LITTLE KING

The worm in the fold. Discoloration on ankle.
Undesired erection. From whence comes
    this inverse fountain?
As we study our fair gaze in convex mirror,
Hades is behind, holding an hourglass over   [Obliques,
    our blond nordic locks.   Numéro Spécial,
His other talon pulls a veil across our pubes. Hans Bellmer,
                                              1975]
Dante rushes to the scene
and is frozen there, an image,
as is the infant, tangled in veil's end.
Under everything, an inverse fountain,
surface translating into surf.
My skeleton longer than my life. My?
"Yeah," says the worm in the fold, "my—
we share the word, making its blank bold.
I'll turn you on while watching rape, deplete you
over your darling, or transform your nose
into scrotum hanging De Sadely out of what's
    inserted into your face.
On the isle of the unconscious
(around which ego breaks its waves),
bodies are in constant exchange.
Think of me as the king of your hill,
the termite soul all your members serve,
Grand Central Station compressed into a fanged snout,
or the identity ego must trust to get the tomatoes
    in the sack,
drive home without collision and turn on the flame.
The ego, desperate for autonomy, is the rector of
    long division.

41

All else is supremely indifferent to your fate,
and rather carelessly rowing through you
or bowing in you, or playing pinochle on
what is left of the rags pounded out on your crib,
not the Maple but the Diaper Rag
I crawl in while I crawl out
grace of my giving you something to loathe
while the two of us gamble for a spell.
Shell game. Bell game. Look up! and you'll see
the dance on the isle as a bell tower
deliriously pregnant with ringing,
as I, the Quasimodo of your being,
pound up and down from below."

The worm thought for a moment, then added:
"You saw Spicer and Crane going after Wright's liver—
Wright is now nursing from one of the udder formations
in this poem, seeking strength to chew into this energy
and, like a hermit crab, enshell the poem,
turn it into *his* dwelling place.
'Influence' plays little part in this—those great dead
you hold in imagination are thus contained,
they act upon the poem as emanations.
The poem draws strength from such containment.
It is those you have not read, or have dismissed,
who, upon finding you asleep, attack.
Think of the poem as a translucent termite hill—
which white ants are words? which ones ghosts?"

[for Herbert Lust]

42

WHITE NIGHTS
the peelings of day

on my back in the dark,

   mind swept by garish balls,
as if on Vincent's table,
deep pockets
refuse to yield their clue,
or cue. The slender dark hisses:
"You have your own deep pockets
in which a little salt water
contains the zoa of your form"

     to let insomnia chatter.
          night flightery, greeps
tossed up, may be a timbrel fairies beat
   to create a buttercup of sound.

in semi-sleep one writes in strait jacket.

      All night
      I was Epeira
      retying and extending
      what I drew forth
      all day.

              Revision, the stamina of vision.

I AWAKE AT 5 AM SEEING A SERBIAN BAYONET
in a Muslim woman's vagina.
Who today is afraid of Hell?
Who lives for beyond his life?
Saddest to think of living only for
one's revenge—on being born? on being?
Saddest is our need for a Pope,
for a religious girdle to contain our
       raging fat.
"She told him she'd just had a hysterectomy"
—no, I won't repeat more here,
isn't Death cruel enough?
Doesn't nature work its cruel lacework
fine enough?
           Symphony of sad songs,
musical trough into which our compacted
revulsion, our anxious bitterness,
drip. I am weaving in, around,
the bayonet fact
    —a porcupine
in my lines tries to shoot spines
into reader heart, anti-cupid,
enraged artist no reader can receive,
as a poet to be a porcupine,
swine and spine, out of sow lineage
to complex my reign as man,
barbed, concealed by whiteblack hair,
connotations ray, prehensile tale,
the spines never fully flee, or hit home,

the swine sheath is never empty,
the rootedness remains here,
no word is fully said.

UNDER LOUSE ARREST

I fear a louse of phantasmagorical energy,
a stallion maggot refusing to be a fly,
          holding all captive,
feeding all, immersing all in contrasoul,
then slaughtering from within.

          *

We are at every moment in swill with nothingness,
          in the awe of chaos bottled
as the blood head of male nuclear destruction.
          The Grail unidentifiable still
because we have not created a common stone
     fluidified with Kali's ichor.

          *

          I am anchored to Sonoran pronghorn,
               to Queensland rat kangaroo,
               to white-headed saki, to you,
               disgusting plague of novelty,
shield against which men have crushed the underworld.

46

AFFIRMATION'S WAKE

---

                            havoc of man
"The world is charged with the ~~grandeur of God~~."
It flies through the night, Blake's worm,
the Treblinka Express, gathers in the dispossessed,
concentration cored into a camp.
Where do men get their fury?
From the theft of womens' power?
Is what we call the abyss
the ensouling of a surrounding *male*festation?

All men carry the perversion of Hopkins' "charged."
"As if the earth under our feet
were
an excrement of some sky"
As if an old, old unlivable were in Missionary Position over
    all that can be taken, gored.

And for all this, there's a sweetness never spent,
a rare freshness that seems,
    in the lamblight of torture,
a mesmerizing shield screening off the full glare
    of what men do.
O infected brightness! Against your turning-milk-
                  swollen breast
      I press my Holy Ghostless head,
         a parody of the Somalian babe
    sucking through her mother air.

EXILES

Wreaths of wild chrysanthemums
drift
   your small, hard breasts.

A pack of newborn windows waits to be fed.

      Blinded, oxen drag
blackened students like distended drums.

Who says metal doesn't scream
one pale thumbprint called the moon?

      Our love
sleigh's iced lake's a wound!

  A panda, in caged Victorian shade,
dreams of tadpoles
   wriggling, searching for green coral.

Your eyes float in their sockets
  like two fish after mating
each swimming its own way.

          [after Bei Dao,
          Duo Duo,
          Gu Cheng
          & Mang Ke]

MET GLANCES
telegraph back.
In ignition, I'm pre-mind.
Then as I look, and observe,
society recontextualizes. The frame is
the parking lot, the Kroger sign,
the 55 square feet of rain forest in a Big Mac,
the Rain Forest Crunch, my grocery sack.

But as our glances hit
that other was game!
The women were back at the nesting hole,
synchronic.
I was a mobile bristle,
with balls for ballast.

AFTER PINDAR

The Siberian Greco-Roman wrestler,
Aztec obsidian embroidered skull,
muscles   plates, or
tectonics,   they say some just collapse at his feet.
Is he
the god-force I feel in Vedran Smailovic,
a member of the Sarajevo Opera, in formal evening attire,
playing outside the bakery where Serbian mortars struck
a bread line in late May, killing 22 people.
Every day, for 22 days, Smailovic braved
sniper and artillery fire to play
Albinoni's *Adagio* in honor of those who had died—

Autumn sings,   in singe with winter's fangs.

CARRION GOSSIP

Turning on the spit, dream basted,
grub for the gods of day,
I am the food that speaks,
rotational, psychotic, a man with a chance
    to so twist,
  of caduceus,
upon my stem,
I am the toad half-swallowed by the garter snake
rearing in glut frenzy
    sporting
like a horned Viking wavy toad legs.

The cockroach. The ache in the crotch.
Rider in everyone's sidecar.
Helmet with 14 legs, king of your hill and mine.
Alert as snail tweezers, siphoning oil
   from the burial bags of the poor.
Visored ghoul befriending the enraged Hell's Angel
   as well as protein-
starved Papillon on Devil's Island.
The cockroach. Pet of the breadbox,
rumba bug with your Dodgem maze of adolescent sinners,
transferring at 4 AM the Tables of the Law
to the maw of electric digestion.

Exactly who is that Lucifer swiveling earthward,

"coming in on a wing and a prayer,"
as if in slow motion—over immense time—

51

once we've killed them off, who then despise?

*

O give in my soul to this back hurtling through space!
It is the Countess B
still wandering the stairwell of male mind,
waiting for breast blood, or
the gamelan of a virgin's fury.

Human nature, which beats its slaves to music,
is composed of arias, behind which:
mounds of dirt enable B to cross from the Pool
    of Dismembered Rose to
her canopied bed, in which the Ghost of a Shark
is the mattress impression of the Other—
"mounds of dirt," indeed,
    Mounds of Carrion Gossip,
to be admitted here, as we Hams
eavesdrop on the opened belly of Central A.

A roach energy tendrils through all attempts
to contain these Countess holdings.
After all, she only murdered 600.
Unlike us, she killed point blank.
Unlike us, she felt her victims' pudendas.
We have placed an ego-impacted purgatory
between computer bank and the peasant shack
in which our victims are tortured.
We have refueled the Somoza of a wasp-caterpillar
    implantation
in the backs of people! we will never meet.

TABLE OF ONE

When I eat alone, I listen to my fork scrape
as if I am being dragged
through a gauntlet of the initiated.

Or am I dragging, coolie-wise,
the rickshaw in which, for centuries,
God's infante has been on world tour?

Then a dread passes through me
that the anima mundi has diminished to
under half left in the bottle. As with Armagnac,
will flatness now take over?

>   Rising through East River
>   like Excalibur,
>   a Crisco-
>   lathered fist.

A FRIENDSHIP

Koki, I keep looking at you
across my skeleton, so as to keep the whole
within grasp. The Hillhurst mansion
   hung with New Year crepe,
your fingers pressing into Beethoven,
a quiet Sunday afternoon, 40 seated
where 200 had romped. Sonata in A^b Major, Op. 110.

Cataclysmic chamber of literally
no world after we go, and no
            way I can be equal to
your having been visited by Death.
Mine is still on a Bergman screen,
an awareness, not a chess presence,
even if I do wear my father's eyeballs
like jester bells attached to my back.

Stripped redbud, have you *anything* to tell us?
You'll come around, spring, how practiced
you'll be for your crumbling!
            Or are you now so seasoned
that your dimension is beyond us?
We, who seem to have only one bend,
oh we, the bundled up,
whose open-endedness is
contingent.
            How use language
in such a way that what it can't do
shows more potently than what it can?

To arm-wrestle on the kitchen table late at night.
As if an hour later, sweet rolls, in the nook,
sunlit Sunday, tentative America, a newspaper,
                    we are guests.

No memory equal to the sibylline structure of the other.
Your musical laugh jiggling
ice cubes over your warm, warm heart,
always a bit off center.
We court a center whose function is to take our good
    and then to kill us.
At ice, art is the key to survival,
God only occurs after person—
                    before person,
the human is constructed out of eating image,
an image eating an image, more primary
than food?
            Lascaux
is the debris of image eating,
            as if Cro-Magnons were bees
buzzed to image.

    Why didn't I tell you this before?
Why didn't I tell myself?

Poetry holds many. But does it hold friendship?

I swallow the mother oyster, and proceed.
You waver in my sight, indecisive
brother emotion. I watch you move toward music
and move away, your vacillation is so real
I sense the extent to which I've murdered vacillation
to do what I've done. Your arabesque hesitation
truer to the world we live in.

            (Koki
the iron shrine of a train whistle,
road groans, cat shriek, 30 feet away as if arctic.

55

You so near, so love and marrow
                    filled with never,
oh my. how not lament myself.
                              You are 3000 miles away
as am I, if I am here,
my statement hangs on this,
the wall
the wall!
the facing non-you of the night,
                    dear friend. Words like fingers
caressing your heels. Into what eternity can I set
                    the madness of illness,
                    irrational   nature
screws love, unknowing bugs copulate in our eyes

You are a stamen
oh you do blossom did do do blossom in my heart
oh is there language to crib to hold
     your forlorn hand?

                    Had you over for an omelette
                    we became friends

I don't want to ode or to elegize you
I want to sensitize these words to your being

You generously enhearthed Caryl
and I, pale flame,
you said: welcome
you said: how rude!
you said sit down at my table for 100
you said be of my family
you said my mother and father are good

North Vermont changed as all of us knew you,
your bookstore window changed, we heard Collard,
     the music in the book
     the book before music

and we arm-wrestled before your stove,
on the floor, then leg-wrestled,
silly way a heterosexual, maybe, engages one
he admires

or maybe not silly
maybe our way of shaking,
Koki, or playing

  as all of us know you
  as you responded to so many.

PICKED UP THE ROTTED DOORMAT
coming apart in my hands, under id the morgan force,
worms here, pile, pour,
a nest—not of puppies! Earthworms,
good things! I could not gaze
at this primal, family scene—what is offensive?
Pinkish maroon, is it—spaghetti?
too close to my tongue? too close to language?
or am I uncovering my parents making me?
For I did pull up the doormat,
    there,   they are writhing,
exposed. It sinks in fast, then slowly,
the internal no longer eternal
    slime begetting slime, the *I am*
stripped of *will be*
and heroic *was*,
                        the present is without skin?
The present is the most buried.
The present is corroded from both ends?

And there is my life under the doormat!

SO BE IT

The suffocating nearness of mother

The more suffocating distance of father

(as he comes forth with a switch,
she retreats)

The lightning distance of mother

The leaden nearness of father

internalized, this seesaw, she in my left eye, he in my right. At the focal point, I helplessly superimpose them. Focus, in Latin, is fireplace. So, at the focal hearth is something burning? Is their primal coupling disappearing or becoming sacred? It would appear that a sole (burnt offering) density is being created
as the Ajna Chakra, located between the eyebrows, the third eye, a two-petaled lotus, encompassing lingam in yoni, "the supreme creative act."
It is miraculous, in fact, that in this third eye I am propellering them, grinding them to a whirr, or swastika, a triskelion consisting of three human legs with bent knees, or tentacles, coiling about a single center. In other instances, the center is a belly, or a Gorgon's face, her turning legs incipient snakes. Or it is two energy streams curving into each other, as in van Gogh's "Starry Night," the spiral form which Wilhelm Reich called "cosmic superimposition," in his eyes "*the* basic bio-physical form."

Before the hooked cross, before linear corners, angles might have been suggested by two superimposed curling lines, with one line tending toward straightening (male), the other tending toward self-enclosing (female). Before semen was thought to be primary in conception, the straight line, or slit, may have been in the service of the enclosing one, may have been semi-enclosed by it, the ensemble making the form of the earliest engraved vulvas. This image evokes a very early form of the labyrinth, a simple, female labyrinth, into which the male entered, swerved, sacrificed a part of himself, and withdrew.

At the point that the instrumental role of semen in conception was assumed, there was a massive redistribution of female and male dominance in favor of the latter. Idealistically, one might wish that a reciprocity between the sexes had set in, an equalization of creative potential. However, as we know all too well today, nothing like this happened. Emboldened by the discovery of his so-called primacy, the male line of the simple labyrinth broke through the cul-de-sac, or swerve area, and rather than turning and withdrawing, pushed on and on, as if to resolve entering through unending penetration. The breaking point became an intersection, or a center within, the nucleus for the labyrinth as we know it today, in which a life and death struggle takes place, and from which, even if victorious at the center, the victor may never emerge but continues to wander the winding paths.

Once the male line broke through in this pictograph, the formerly dominant self-enclosing line of the simple labyrinth, having lost its interior magnet, so to speak, lost its shape, and began to wander, branching off to become the maze space of the hero's testing. At a fundamental layer of psyche, male and female are as two night crawlers moving over and around each other, blindly searching, unaware that their point of superimposition is the center of centers out of which and around which mythological conflict emanates.

Practically speaking, over thousands of years, we have contained these crawlers and set them revolving in the third eye. Yet our attentions wander, we are more often than not out of sync with what we most desire, men and women know and do not know what the other requires . . .

So when I look into my eyes, the pork work of my parents, disintegrated in the irises years ago, becomes a broken and living labyrinth, full of gaps, collapsing and continuing in these fragmentary constructions.

[Placements IV]

STRATA

Apes treading reddened surf
as carnivores snarl at the water's edge.
Bipedal cycling starts up in the Miocene.
At any moment the air may catch fire.
Beach is the lion gate.

Face-before-birth, strangled bog man,
lodged in a nexus so stratigraphic
nickle and stars piled into his vocabulary.

I lifted this face-before-birth
out of its vulval coffin,
lifted the cord away from his neck . . .
skull rich in tentacular moss,
skull infused with hemorrhaging mantas.

To slit open sin is to discover being.
The poem, as the earth, rises and performs creation.
The barest mental line fills in, a rump, a face,
implications cut across the sound shellac.

In Cousteau's beam: Bud Powell
                sits, yogic,
            drawing out his colon,
            each finger a pallbearer,
                        a fish on puppy legs
                trundling along   deeper
        than where life
                    had been thought to live.

UNDER WORLD ARREST

With a bite, the apple eater is surrounded.
Is this one sprayed? Near Eve's teeth marks,

the poison is most intense.
So Original Sin flares in any act,

in the act of the mind
world arrest asserts itself,

the Garden is re-performed, and angels,
blotched yellowish-white, arms linked,

move a lariat loop through consciousness,
charged to do God's thickening.

Inside the sinew arithmetic,
arathattacks. Healable, in rind.

At core, the irrefutable,
sleep-infested, early marble:

   God is moving over.

A CROSS SECTION OF THE INCARNATION

Christ's ear, fermented in van Gogh's absinthe, finally arrived—
said to be a few meters larger than the Yokohama Buddha. After
several days of sawing, we worked our way through the conch.
When we dragged the auditory canal apart, we were able to
observe a cross section of the Incarnation. Working from auri-
cle to labyrinth, this is what we observed:

Outer Lens shells of Composition B, followed by bulged
detonation waves, next to inclusions of Baratol, which had
curved and merged with an inward-driving sphere, followed by
a second shell of solid fast Composition B and a wall of dense
uranium tamper, followed by the nickle plating of the pluto-
nium core, which had been squeezed into an earhole with a
tiny initiator at the center, whose designed irregularities were
mixed with beryllium and plutonium. Conditions within the
earhole resembled the state of the universe moments after its
first primordial explosion.

Once our scientific eyes turned inward, we perceived the
cross section in a different way: Composition B became Count-
ess B; the detonation waves were frozen, stampeding horses,
in whose nicked flesh were Panic inclusions, followed by an
inward-driving pressure on the dreamers' hearing, whose fan-
tasies were mixtures of wilderness and cultures, truffled, as it
were, by bits of ax blades. When we inquired into the nature
of this ax-embedded hearing, we were riddled with sword-
embedded stones. What had from a scientific viewpoint looked
like an earhole, now appeared to be the dissolution of hearing
and experiencing, satori, or the place of origin.

The ground vanished. We were soaring, all of us, cling-
ing to our great, severed prize. We were, we wee ones, like
hairs billowing, drifting the abyss, much of which had been

concentrated into the object of our clinging. Gradually, we struggled up and then down into the fossa of the antihelix, and found shelter. It was in this moonpond, by firelight, that we penned these Lilliputian speculations:

At the moment the Word became Flesh, or enfleshed itself, the impaction of energy was tremendous, and the conditions for the discovery of fission were established.

Surely a Last Judgement is at hand. The Face of Hell is the elimination of nature; the Face of Heaven, God's reinvention of Himself as "nature."

Quotational Reality is the new Purgatory making each desire artificial.

Not "a nightmare from which I am trying to awake," Joyce, but the daymare in which Venus, flash-frozen and vacuum-packed, sprints, in place, toward us.

VENUSBERG

Her hub is too inconstant, too
       shape-changing.
She rises from the sea, "foam-born,"
—but it is great that she
can change, for without her protean lay,
men would have nailed her to her litoral,
made her literal, destroyed her
  for you and me—

a whorled shell,
is she the animal within?

A headless bison, shaped
like a ventricose shell,
embracing an identical bison—
the two, like human lovers,
forelegs torso wrapped,
on and of a reindeer antler—

In Kafka, when one sentence sets forth,
another starts out from the far
side of the original thought.
It is like watching venery approach venereal,
while, at another angle, venom
has sighted venial. When such words fuse,
they thirst in us, thus do not fuse,
because we are fission incarnate.

It is we who are fleeing Venus,
Venus's sons, venison, staggered

66

by the force that wraps into form,
the retainer, at the epicenter of phenomena,
the grip that holds ventricose
bison and faceless woman in a single throe.
   She also rises from the rock,
fat spindly lady, milky cob
in the birth channel of our palm,
the spinster born at Laussel,
holding high a drinking horn?
for a lover? a killed hunter brother?
Does it contain blood? and if so,
menstrual, or of slaughter?
Is it, torn from a larger animal form,
a spoke of *ven-*?
   What she holds is ripped
venerability,
                    we hang
from her upheld horn.

        "The most beautiful of women
        handed him the beaker.
        His heart and mind
        shuddered with sweet horror.
        He emptied it to the last drop,
        then the dwarf at the door said:
        now you belong to us,
        for this is Venus Mountain."

THALASSA VARIATIONS

She lay back upon the sea, fully buoyed.
As he hovers over, waves churn
as if to unstill her. She is Caryl
not Caryl, no Caryl pervading Caryl—
not his mother but redressed
as his other, as if the labyrinth were falling apart,
and the central
receptionist, the goal buried
beyond the bull's-eye, were surfacing.

Visions of canals enweb his mind.
What he is in, hovering over, is not
without her. The air is moist,
sprayed by plumes of iridescence.
He is, arms outstretched, legs held together,
a Y chromosome facing its X
on the Z of nature's altar.

She reaches up and pulls him down—
he is small, constructed
about his mouth eager for nipple.
He sucked to feel the inner tent, his intention
harden, the circus of fledgling nerves
in which gnats were juggling, sharks
were swallowing fire. Now he knows:
as he nursed, the phylum was astir.
Teeth like penile sprouts appeared,
imitations of the erectile world.

A kiss, and volumes fall apart,
for the entering is not ineffable—
say it, educated shark,
male with a cleaver in your fist
not a fist, but ferny fingers,
Aladdin's foreplay on the lamp of the sea.
In each covering, the mirage of paradise flashes,
semaphore or accordion, in her massive
ballroom bail-out of our spleen.
Of course it is bitter, this need to be bitten off,
to castrate in her grove.
The child masturbated in an anal war
distant from the source of capital,
his scythe moving through nutriment,
as if he were not anchored to her demise.

Wallace Stevens, it is her sex that makes
the sky acutest at its vanishing,
forms the holy V, her grape cluster altar.
Inside her, thus inside metaphor,
he digs the genital tension on her walls,
her fauna relief canal, as when the Ice Age,
freeze-girdling the lower body,
squeezed some image paste into our heads.

O clasper frog, in your embrace:
the catastrophe of life on land!
Although he shudders,
how forgetful he is of what she entubed
to convex and, over aeons,
reshape from cloacal assault.
Is that the source of his detachment?
Unable to detach, he deflates—only sperm
springs beyond the finish line.
Reptilian instant! As his infant
would've penetrated breast to be
back inside, a god,
so his amphibian, stranded,

tried to regain liquidity
via another's invaded flesh.
And below intrauterine repose?
Penis as sinless fish, traveling
its origin, grounded as he moves.
A hundred fathoms below,
mother skeleton wavers,
five hundred fathoms deeper,
a salamander skull is ooze.
Uprush of glacial
blackness that like a corkscrew
ventilates his serpentine hypnosis,
as if his body were whirled by mother spectre and,
in Escher opposition,
active strands of void.
In fourfold peristalsis,
he is a tree filled with furies,
whose trunk seems skinny,
whose avocados feel immense.

How gorgeous she is!
How much more than a divining rod he is,
the two of them snailentailed
on the genius of the sea—yes,
the waves stay buoyant,
and if they can see through osmosis,
the glass-bottomed
depth of embrace will reveal
carousels of interior drink.
The father of his erection is a crocodile.
Cloacal separation into
intestine and urethra—speak
of duality!—was first
suffered by a kangaroo.
Within the ransacked, still
intact, human midden,
the zodiac pauses—an anatomical
ferris wheel has taken them up,

then dipped them into
a quiet, seething gale.
Yesterday, he was a raper mole
acrawl with dessicational mystery.
Today, half in ice, half hybrid,
as if a child had scrawled him.
Imago? Or feathered serpent?
To strike. To wander.
Mind, where does it *not* come from?

With manganese-smeared finger,
pigmenterrial. No longer merely masturbating,
but negative hands. No longer merely hallowing vulva,
but hollowing cupules. On eye-stalks
to roam Le Portel, to squirm,
on back, into a sarcophagal cul-de-sac,
head pressing end, to go beyond end,
to engrave in rock, inches above,
a stag, whose head, also pressing back,
thus miming the engraver,
bells into the end: *image is*
the imprint of uncontainable omega,
                    life's twin.

THE CHAOS OF THE WISE

Why this yearning to travel?
More, this deeper yearning to return?
Falcon intuition. Human foible loop.
At the far end of the drive to flee from one's feet
there is psyche. Who is strong enough
to take up residence there?
Imagination desires circularity,
not repetition. Psyche wants recurrence,
on each swing the path to deepen,
a rattler raga, wants to uroboros herself.
Or take Pech-Merle:
                              the rockwall bears an image
which presses in a fraction of an inch.
Someone's squatting there, drawing horse and bison
close as she distances them,
as she works the primordial hourglass,
a double bellows, or butterfly.
            Wall as thorax:
out there one wing, in here another.
Imagination as dorsal lines superimposed,
one crossing another, making a statement
imprisoned by the ochre on her finger—
she can't press through the wall she is to penetrate,
a finger in the void, a traveling semen-travesty.
Chaos's lips purse to suck on her plunger-finger.
Her drawing times her, as here each word
                  has its worm ward.
To be underborn in the chaos of the wise,
to take the oath of the abyss
verging on being of the physical world!

All the I/s huddle, as if, as one,
they could remain in goddess doorway all their lives
—what terror! what delight! Psyche wonders:
might there still be one great mother with everyone
daisy-chained to her rich hole? Do we sink
Hades and Persephone into Hades
for a sensation of life wedded to its origin?

HOMUNCULA

[by Horrah Pornoff]

1

WHOSE FEATHERS DO
not glisten as her wings

shake with pain?
Whose bird is not hit?

Whose head is not hidden
under her absent lover's body

in the box she has been
placed in, her office,

the head in which she
waits for someone to heal her?

Whose ankle is not
banded with a name?

2

SHIT,
we sisters never had a table.

We had
only a test tube, held vertical, history.
Like sulphur we clouded,
epanadiplosic.

Straight up, the Matterhorn
god-climber whose rose
we swore to, Germanic,
polishing our endless
ant-egg linkage,
to sanitize our blood,
thus mortal, thus mortality-denying.

From the heights What
looked down on us, in pity to
pry apart our vertical to
a V, to name us,
as if my sister whose feet
are hinged to mine, must be added
for us to equal Thee?

3

I LIVE IN THE SKY
off the hero's palm.

At times, his crusts
are feasts which camouflage

his size as mine,
he seems to be within my grasp,

a glass surf board
between myself and the roar . . .

he is. Intransitive.
Kaleidoscope of nays.

4

TO BE AN UDDER DRIPPING IN THE LIE.
To feel acutely the size of trees,
the cutaneous test of wind,
to return on the body
spoken, as if in rim.

And to be in touch, womanic,
to lean back into the noun.
But to be suffix, mother, to have other
buried behind an m,
I lie

in

her lie,
a supporting beam in the Tomb of M.

5

TO THE EXTENT THAT I AM INJECTED,
I suffer absence, of God and of animal.
Yet to the extent that I am injected,
I can use absence, I can crawl
through my misery at the same time
I wrap myself in its ancient folds—
there I would suffer even worse, or
I should say, I do—I marry that suffering here.

6

TO LISTEN TO EACH MENSTRUAL
period confined caked hut board,
in the desquamation of a mucous view—
infinintestinal redemption
footbound to a woman in Asia,
barebound to myself,
Jewish, trench aware, sun and moon expectant.

7

WHEN POETRY ACTUALLY OCCURS,
the particle flow between the mind and
the ceaselessly cabling other is monitored.

Glazed with the effort
to keep wet in the kiln,
I am handed out, homuncula.

8

I AM MY FATHER'S ONLY UNBORN DAUGHTER.
I gave birth to my mother and am responsible for her death.

Someone who believes that at least one part of her
is immortal is at loose in this room,
some hag who has set her peat on fire,
who, as if they are cosmetics,
is doodling with the fumes.

9

I CAME UPON MY MOTHER, AN UNBORN CHILD.
Her rimless letters floated before
the animal wall I had erected to see her by.
Out of serpentine repetition,
I sought to be doubled again,
to watch her decomposition compose . . .

Do you remember being born?
Then, were you?
Do you remember willing dying?
Then, must you?

All of the French Legion has been withdrawn.
The sands relax, now only under camel power,

and the no birth no death feeling that occurs
is my eaten-out navel in my hand unravelling . . .

10

TRYING TO OPEN THE OTHER,
I panicked and went for my towel,
winding it up, as in the past, tight between my legs,
pulling it up curtain-tight, like a grinding stripper,
trying to gag my skull . . .

11

AND IF AFTER SO MANY GODS,
the word covering the force
were to tear, and the force itself not exist!
If after so much prattle about eternity,
eternity were to disappear—
might we, if weaned of the infinite,
realize nature
as we know it is kaput?

The greatest insult is to be
within words, pressed to the backside of words
whose other sides are in actual
contact with what the words are said to mean . . .

an insult, worse, a folly,
even worse, the knowledge
that engenders self-hate.
Is it any wonder, then,
that people back their cradles up
to their tombs
to dump in life untouched?

12

UNDER DEATH
as if in nickel

the actual
ledge of the sickle.

Scythe,
you are my seed.

13

BEING PULLS
     as if to magnet
I, filing, iron.
          I piss,
like all women,
          rust,
because my letters cannot yet porn out all
     the masculine hardware.

14

TO FEEL THE EARTH'S CURVE
under palm,
neither flat
though flatness is felt
as the mean
between the inverted bowl
I make of earth and
my palm's arch.

To touch, then,
is to feel hollow,
to imagine a womb
insinuation in the gossip
between plates, like us,
laminating their lamentations.

15

X HAS INVITED ME TO LUNCH TODAY.
While I sit in my skirt, he's in the Hungry Tiger can,
speed-zipping his fly. High on that special freedom,
he returns. Picking joke upon joke from the letchwater
always within pun reach to any mind.

As if I have a skull down there!
Around which he's tied a tiny shower curtain.
Lobster? If I could only tie up
the bottom of my skirt and still walk.
Or Steak? If I could only lift, and riding
the hardness of my thought fly point-blank into his zippered
    illusion,
that wall between navel and prick Dante called "the holy
    vacuum,"
while he picked paradises off Beatrice,
like fleas, nibbling each before her hungry eyes.

He said "vacuum" to me to bring up
the metaphysic in my floorboards.
Unable to raise himself, he wants me to pup up
his tent for him, to Via Negativa him with desire.
Poor pupa sex, the non-entity
I am brassiered in, bewildered by so much in my hymn.

16

THE OFFICE, FILLED WITH CHINESE LAUGHTER,
is Western chop suey at 5,
the hour the bull,
lamed by hunger, is prodded into time,
and my heritage,
behind its spectatorial fan,
vegetally perspires for
the blood imagination of the matador—

or so it appears
in the eyes of the woman who watches me—
she unfurls her huipil
like a red Saint Vitus flag,
and steps outside me a little after 5.

Corrida of an intelligence, then,
for the whole spilled athanor of a time
I believed in tied to, I-lust
to lie out, Horrah Pornoff,
Procrustian receptionist
wedged into carmine shoes and checked
in the Chinese box maze
of the world Greyhound Station.

17

TEHUANA FRIDA BY VICTORIAN HORRAH.
Two bodies linked veinriverwise to the desire to be double
enough to live—and Frida does truly live, with her insect smile
and her locked woolyworm eyebrows.

Her greeting card balloons would spiral off happy birthdays
but stayed on to float folksong melodies over Frida and Diego
in the rimless forever of a fixated bird skull I see held by Frida's
fragile pelvis which needed to be cupped! yes, as Christ cupped
the Grail and drank from it, all of his head except his lips
covered by eyes.

Frail, frail Frida, borne in like scarlet bougainvillea strewn
across a casket.

The darts in your spine reangled the cantina word-drapery.

Your insolent courage forced Surrealism to frame your
honest face.

18

THE GLISTEN ON SUNSET AT 7
as the neon turns on geek
prayers to Apollo.
Appeals. Slogans. As if wounds were throwing off
    their bondage minks.

The weather report: Hail tonight,
with brickbats approaching the incubators.

19

COMPRESSED CHARWOMAN—I said to a fire hydrant—
phial embedded with Aladdin,
4-spigoted glimpse of kneeling woman,
Isis searching for her lost sponges,

genius of contraction, foetus
awaiting a fix, most shot through
addict, arm thrust in lysol,
patriarchal inhaler, rib

bent into a knee, tappable,
uncontactable, waiting to serve,
O squat riveted dependability
in deathrow to an alarm.

20

TO HEAR THE "DESS" IN GODDESS,
the Odessa layers of the suffix of God.

In order to desperm the loom,
I now respell Gyneandrogy.

"dess, so auxiliary to God,"
head dress, as if we
are the hair of the head of God.

We are his slugway.
He is whelped in our slime.

He, immortalized in the atmosphere,
while the jugular pumps below,
below the queen's tiara,
below her veil-hung stable,
even below her blinded,
lip-clenched
hornet.

21

I AM SURROUNDED BY LAUGHTER
as Stonehenge
by barbed-wire, an active moat,
an ugly
value affirmation. Let's call it water,
this bale of noise,
crept into, has it veins? If so,
a heart?
I want to rebend the doubled-over men,
to see if they spring back,
or fire back and forth, on the fulcrum of laughterpain.
An inch inside a sneer,
there's a cliff;
below, the damned are braiding the flames.
So the man cracking up
has his hair on fire, and
he's trying to shake the brimstone into my eyes!
(Until now I've worn goggles
when I ventured out into humanity.
It's time to turn my eyeballs into targets,
to examine the extent to which the horizon
penetrates my vertical assumption of the crown)

22

TWO SKELETONS INTERDANGLE MY OWN.
The one of Red Bone is very old, very
permeated with ochre mother.
The one of Black Bone is very burnt, very
sick of altar consummation.
It yearns to be packed and posted
by my own of White Oklahoma Bone,
its vine, its sustaining
virgin wall.
         And so,
I awake to my desire for friction of any kind,
with anyone, and to my desire for half of myself,
perhaps a woman, unmet,
perhaps a figure of snow
whose only point of contact is a salted cinder.
Love, thus, might be a state
where I live with only that unmet half,
never meeting who I would be living through.
I could walk up to a stranger I know well
and present myself as single and split.
Then he, or she, or perhaps the snow animal
I approach, would, with its cinder,
or perhaps with its tongue, divide me again
(I would be a touch that soft)
and through each finite division, love
would, with each split, be
more accurately defined.

23

ETERNITY IS THE GREATEST CONSUMER.
It buys from everyone her
being, his life as it were.
The seller gazes off
empty-shelved, into the sanctimonious blue.

I know that if I drop to my knees,
I worship not only what I sold
but what is packed above the fruited plain.

That consumptive beyond is watching,
wanting me to kneel, placing
fingers inside brocaded poppets, making
god fun at the end of my weaning
(man an incomplete woman,
woman an over-complete man,
nature a caricature of person).

I have left a concrete case of nothing
and so, check in, while nothing unpacks
clamp and razor, a traveling salesman
who runs a tool stand on the side.

Perhaps, while I lie in state,
he will screw back in all my treasures?

24

LAST NIGHT I HAD INCARNATION FOR DINNER.
As I swallowed Logos and projected
my own paradoxical garnishes,
I became technological flesh.

Nature went on welfare
and lined up on screen
(I was now to tend her who used to
so indifferently restore and injure me).

My salvation consisted in buying junk
through which God's purity was
ceaselessly revealed.
Then Christ appeared in designer Transcendence.

He would have joined me, had I not
already joined Him. For comic relief,
Christ begged me to lash what was left of us.
I flogged, bridally.

Switching channels, I saw,
through His eyes, all was empty space
crowded with news and immaculate death.
—Then I heard a bell toll

as if 2000 miles away. Zeros whirled
through pagan earth, Before-to-After,
boring an axial hole. New zero hour!
Birthday gift—for the infinite.

25

GROUPIE TO A HOLY GRAIL,
some might say. And it is true:
I still have one finger on a manger,
but one in which the fit is Siamese,
where prostitutes and surgeons
are packed among the circling wiseguys.

Given such Gnostic democracy,
it would be foetal to ask for strength
—which is exactly what I will do.
When they cease tossing meat into my bowl,
I'll crawl back under Hathor's dugs
                              whose liquor
will more than suffice for the yugas
                              when, in hell,
I'll be my own fork, meal, and stove.

THIS IS THE SAVANNAH ON WHICH I WORKED
through gender.
                        Free of both life and death,
I look through your eyes reading,
                ravenous for your mind.

Between flight and hyena, I speculate on the kill
from the viewpoint of ascension,
a nail
        vertically afloat over

    the gravity of its hole

            pullulation.

                                    [1975–1993]

LEAKY VESSELS

Said Pinocchio to Cinderella:
our stories used to be separate,

now my room has partially tumbled into yours.
We enter each other like kids on a spree,

doomed to crash eternity and
feeling right at home. But content and meaning,

replied Cinderella, have become a stable
where a perfunctory mating occurs.

I thought it would be more interesting to meet you,
rather than running through

my own story for the umpteenth time.
Fine, said Pinocchio, but because you are here,

I'm no longer interested in brooding upon
my manhood-to-be, nor upon my wooden youth.

My story hangs through your carriage side,
an ice-cube melting.

And mine, cried Cinderella,
an ice-cube invaded by your ruddy hearth!

NEGATION'S PARTICLES,
earth surface: pressure cooks
   as the mind dances like rice.
No wonder Language Poetry,
            no wonder.

MORTIFIED CITIZEN

My soul's grief is
it persuades no one. On ancient scales,
it underweighs a feather. Here,
the window of imagination is always
blood spattered. I see through the blood.
I see, through the blood.
"I see through." —The Blood.

What *does* the soul want . . .
Does it want to intercede between us
and these Kuwait morgue mutilated faces,
to stitch "the knowledge of the beauty of death"
into us, so that such a suture
becomes a sutra within us?

George Bush, said to be most present,
now intensifying his invisibility,
just urged me to leave the sphere of affirmation
and to take up negativity as the post-
historical course of man.

Bush, who never took my hand when I was little,
now closing me, like an account,
just explained that upon his ascension,
the tabulability of things actually ended
(As compensation
he has painted my eyes with secularity,
hung zeros from my lips).

Never to forget: by thrusting an urn of blazing semen
    into the female dark
the Husseins and Bushes have blackened the wall of nature,
    and,
into BC
        AD, split the human heart,

        2 warring outposts,
        4 severed arms around a pit
        attempting to grasp
        zero in its self-embrace.

IF I WERE JOHN HEARTFIELD
I'd replace the rattler heads of Coatlicue
with Hussein and Bush, George's right eye
    Saddam's left, bringing
Her head into our era,
as their tongues explore
without kissing, lobster palpitating lobster
—as Vallejo saw it, 1937—"atrocious microbe,"
below culture
           over Kuwait
phantomatic caterpillar body soft as dark red smoke.

"Saddam should feed his people"

His PEOPLE ?
Harsh peep hole
TV oil gulls
Trash flea skulls
Bash knee hulls
O our people
Our *horror*

Street grief in Baghdad trough
Green meat rags coughed
"For the life of your car go Gulf"
Kill for energy

CNN: "Iraq's colossal fortifications"
"artillery powerful beyond our imagining"
"vast stocks of chemical and biological weapons"
(wave after wave of Americans to be mowed down
by Iraqi tanks buried in the sand!)

BBC: Slaughter of conscripts
"deprived of food and water for days,
with inadequate clothing and third-rate equipment"
hiding in holes

Gulf no-War
"state terrorism on a colossal scale"
"It's almost as if you were turning on the light
in the kitchen at night and the cockroaches begin to run,
and we kill them"

106

We engine honed bowlers
We bowling through flesh
We cleanasa whistle
Dump it over there
Their rumps our gore cloud

Wipe out the trauma of war
Turn it into entertainment
The Disneylands on which our fancy feeds
"Norman our huggable Desert Storm Teddy Bear . . .
plush and loveable . . . ready to storm into your home
and right into your heart"

In sleet, without shelter,
to hold one's half-burned child
Goddamn you Bush,
could I but cut your eyes with the living razor
you've made of that Kurdish child

Can we live without an enemy?

"At what point
does starvation of eighteen million people
take precedence over our attempts to remove
one man from power?"

BASRA HIGHWAY

I can't get out of my embrace
Iraqi conscripts scrambling out of tanks,
having waved white flags
    Called a "withdrawal" (not a "retreat")
to justify our rockets crisping them.

If I didn't have to watch faces peel back,
could I press the button?
Dickey's "Firebombing,"
                high on distance.
    Can't get out of my embrace
  the distance, Dis stance,
        hell pause between
an us, a them, in which cruelty is neutralized.

Can't get these drowning-in-flame ones out of my life,
can't get them deep enough into my embrace,
can't get these phantoms out of my scrotum,
can't carry them on and into and through you,
can't transform their pain into grief,
  my grief into my liquid,
can't whiten my blood with this sorrow

    Oh pus millipede with breasts of blood
this mass I enshare you with
this word mire,
        coffined word
        curdled word
can't get this briar word through my urethra.

108

COPULATION'S DEPTH
is bounded by an alarm
—the planet's on fire!—
the news rushes through,
all hydrants on.

Burning Water. Aztec
conversion—sun
plucked from a groin.
As if for an instant,
my heart came—

blood's blossom
set in cream.

IN BEING SURROUNDED BY

her arms and legs,

                      all nature suddenly
come to visit, one is,
as marrow is, as pith. It is then the angel
enters one's back, proceeds through
one's penis, exiting the beloved's back.
I have never seen my angel's face.
I *have* seen her back rocketing away,
    her fibrous outstretched wings
in that blackness where conjoined parents
                   are molecules.

BLOODROCK

If they wonder why I write of menstruation,
tell them this: I thirst for the moment
a female hominid turned
and faced her partner.
In that moment, Dōgen and Wilhelm Reich were meshed,
"face-to-face transmission,"
the turning of the chair
to face the patient on the couch
Oestrus unbound, a new significance or
the first significance of blood,
a twin for nature,
81,000,000,000,000,000,000 ton
body of the moon emblazoned in her uteral
wall, shedding her heretofore
only purpose: to procreate.
Bloodrock. Spontaneous arousal.
What she projects into me as she bleeds is king,
kin, kunne, mental child of cunt.
I enter her bleeding as the man
she is forming in her mind
       measure*men*t
          *men*sureable
          *men*suration
      com*men*surate
       di*men*sion
       im*men*sity
      nou*men*on
I am clasped that firmly
my "mens" my "menos"
my masculinity is the product of her vise,

111

spiral axis at whose peak is the homuncular tree,
whose Fallopian branches I once wore
        under cuckold
        under Satan
        under Shiva
    under "dancing sorcerer"
as her Horned God.
                    One tragedy, as man,
is the melt down of these branches
into the brain, divinity based on semen.
God Creating Man thrusts a finger out of a brain-like
Michelangelo mass, as if it all started there (he said,
pointing at his head)—
on a secondary level, it did,
but the source of the projection is not within me,
the source is her massive bio-
swerve, her turn within and to me.

SOME FUGAL LUBRICATION

"the Horned one, Cernunnos, was represented in the cross-
legged position of a yogi" horned cross-legged
Drachenloch, "Dragon Lair" 85,000 BCE
        at the basis of mind,
       a severed animal head—
at Drachenloch the rudiments,
          cave bear thighbone
twisted in, between cheekbone and cranium,
lodged there, making an X, Jolly Roger,
the bear's body simplified,
          compressed in the skull,
fixed there, the bone now a wand,
to capture = to conjure, off the head
no longer "head" but throne,
coitus reconstructed, marrow-filled bone
replaces the great semen-marrow brain mass
(which Neanderthal probably ate,
then went back in, for void? screwing in
the cranium space where brain'd been),
semen reconstructed, is semen
          soul heading off?
Väinämöinen, be with me here, help me unpack
the psychic space of this Dragon Lair skull.

    There is a loom in this skull
whose mental strands in furious singing
attempt to fill semen-marrow bereft space.
Around this throne, Death has assembled
         flocks of roaches.
Within this skull, mental winches raised

113

the body of the bear, until only two bones,
crossed, could be seen.   Skull
                              Crossed Bones,
buccaneer at the rim of consciousness,
flag of the slave ship, for
the seizing of souls makes appetite for more,
ruddy peril of life based on soul seizing,
O greatest peril, the brother of an Iglulik shaman
      said to Rasmussen,
human food consists entirely of souls—

at Drachenloch, the chakra impulse of coronation,
the raising of the (now) lowered body
   into a skull house,
                          coronation's brother
is decapitation,   Sacred Head
about which billions of roaches genuflect,
like samurai.
                  The calamity at Drachenloch
of depth-charge proportions,   to go off
throughout histories as people pack
bodies into the abattoirs of their heads,

apparently simple move of
merely a thighbone inserted,
fixed, can't be twisted out,
coital impress can't be dislodged
                  from severed head
without destroying mentation's crown,

the core of a to-be-constructed bomb?
      Pack this primal ignition kit
inside slabs of rock, build a chest
(which they did) to protect—
            in which to consecrate
this piracy, then set it against
Drachenloch's red ochre-smeared backwall,
operatic display of Death enwombed,

114

set into the most uteral part of the cave,
to fertilize the future? At this moment,
Neanderthal must've had future tense.

   As foetus to womb,
   loaded bear skull to the earth,
ah, when will you go off,
    savage vision of our roach-like
boring
   into every haunt of soul—
the earth pregnant with X,
cross-legged, lotal. Not where id was
ego shall be, X it out, X in:
            where brain was,
magic thighbone shall be,
seas will writhe under the banner of Vomito Negro,
seesawing the bone in and out,
bone viol,
   rape inherent in this spectral music,
         buried in unconscious silt
the enthroned skull of the hibernator
                (from whose den
babies mysteriously issue in spring

HUMBABA

The man whose face is composed of entrails
is honest about the labyrinth—
its spill and its anti-spill are hydrant in his gaze
—if it is a gaze (the pinhole eyes of Jack Spicer,
dawn headlights in Leningrad ambering through).
Humbaba wears his dilemma as his puss,
he has a puss, not just a face, but the pus
under, the pile-driven confusion under mask.
No emergence can occur other than through his pores.
All seek Humbaba in any met face—
all seek a labyrinth man to lead through
what for the baby croc is more and more mother,
recombining shells.
                              Humbaba wears a fortress
in his brow, he is a weight-lifter
whose power is concentrated facial timber
(Should we surround Schwarzenegger with praise?
                              Or with dynamite?)
Humbaba has charisma, charisma is a labyrinthine
block.
              Your need for affirmation pulls you in.
Humbaba is the resistance to getting out.
Humbaba lies in wait as the encirclement's core.
Humbaba cannot be taken by storm.
              Humbaba is the middle wall.

116

LIKE VIOLETS, HE SAID

Jacques Marsal [1925–1988] in dapper suede slippers would lead
us into the darkness of Lascaux. It takes his absence today, our
fourth visit, to say how much his presence determined what
Lascaux is. As one of the discoverers, Marsal remained coated
with the awesome freshness of that tumbling in, lightning-ripped
oak, under which four boys squirmed to arrive. That Marsal
stayed on, nearly 50 years, was a bloom added to the stem of
the cave, and I'm overwhelmed by the difference one person
can make in the personality of a place, not via declaration or
sheer information, but by being folded in, obliquely, wearing
Lascaux, allowing its grace to loom, allowing us, hardly aware
of his movements, our own reading through his light.

> Men spring up like violets
> when needed, Olson said,

and Blackburn, near his end,
lamented the disappearance of a Barcelona
waiter, an old man
who moved so accurately and gently
among the clientele. Paul wrote:
"We do not need to know
anybody's name to love them."

Because of Marsal, I know Lascaux in my heart
like a nearly weightless child
framed by thunder and a bruised, milling sky,
a child standing on the sensation of eternity,
sayable eternity, right under the dust.

[Hotel Cro-Magnon]

117

INN OF SOMEWHERE

When Warne Marsh stepped into a dream, this
was an Incarnation I could love—

who went through Koko a barracuda,
or call it Noh-like swordplay,
lightning-quick shadow shaping,
Last Judgement jack-in-the-boxed graves!

Tonight, I sink into your sound, Warne,
as if into matter alive with knots, hard
as my own blood conundrum—
                          your long silken line,
the metal of your ax burned into your lowing.

[26 January 1988]

THE SKELETONS TALK TURKEY

As autumn's wheaten quilt furls back,
the sleepers are revealed,
drying stalks, the long flutes of the dead
begin their agitated piping:
"Do you know your bounty is in part our work?
Don't you know that cob and bone,
the armatures of your increase, prove us?
Will you not drink mescal through the night
by us, until we share a warped, suicidal pang?
For to forget us is to die from us . . ."

Children, impersonating the dead.
How solitary their shapes under street lamps,
Frankenstein, Little Miss Muffet, wending their way . . .
a month later, in the split-off half of that great,
equinox reunion, wolfing down turkey,
thoughts of the dead: the turkey as he sang
his sad, sad tune, and schoolbook Indians.
O interval rife with smallpoxed and massacred millions!
We use Halloween and Thanksgiving like book ends,
as if to contain their volume. I think of tubercular
Oquendo de Amat's *5 metros de poemas*—
who doesn't dream of a book 5 yards wide containing
all it means to be a Peruvian, an American?

In mourning for those with upturned pots for heads,
millions will converge on Lake Titicaca.
There will be a vast weeping tent in the storms of millennium,
when it becomes turgid that
some are frozen, none are thawed.

119

AT THE HINGE OF CREATION
the blinding light of God bends
to cast its shadow
  (the blanket of dark
in which we toss,
                    this hinge
the Norse called Ginnungagap
"De Vries has interpreted the word *ginnunga*
as associated with the idea of deceit through magic,
with the altering of appearances to mislead the eyes"

Olson, out of Fowler, writes:
"licked man, as such, out of the ice,
the cow" Authumla
comes into being to provide food for Ymir,
"a rich, hornless cow"
licks a god-bug-man out
of a thawing ice rose

Ymir is the hybrid, hermaphroditic,
child of the shape-shifting
gap,
      discovered in the late Azilian?
The first Mesolithian?
For the Norse, Ymir is the back wall—

Ymir is the Upper Paleolithic bridge,
a span of eternity
across which a new "we" sets forth,
                    we are here

120

before we were,   not I, not I,
but my peacock display,

    in the ice mirror beast melt,
one is a fleck in the papillae of a cow's tongue,
  origin recedes,   Authumla is mostly
               lost,
is fog, and snow, my cow is tattered,
  fractal,   is milk, steam,
my cow is a dragon,   she cannot be measured,
    in the beast melt down
I am language out on the dragon's tongue,
            anything
  can be cabbie,
          the weals on Francis Bacon's
back are toad glands,   by which
visionary semen issues from his brush.

AT LABASTIDE

We were without a key, and it was pouring as we sloshed ginger-
ly down to the slope leading to the base of the ravine and the
entrance to Labastide. My heels dug into the sog, bright red
beetles were out, dripping ferns, dead leaves.

It was a Rimbaud afternoon, the gate was locked, but I was
to see in the soaring rockwall facing the slope more than I might
have, had we figured out how to jimmy the lock.

At a certain point, rain penetrates the mind, one becomes
part of the gush, a crippled brook, heaving waves, crying, ejacu-
lation form a lotus of imagination in which, a happy drenched
elf, the loosened one sits, double to himself, in embrace, a funny-
looking four-legged egg, all tendril and crevice. The rockwall
bubbled nature-pressed fists into my eyes, a slime of pearls,
scarlet crawlers, violet-tan lichen in fans and cones, a fresh rub-
blework so old
    I belonged instantly
    to Chez Maître Paul,
    I was the goose in the cocotte, a streak of snail graffiti, a
self-infecting gaze into the quilted spongework percolating in
the rain . . .
    I belonged instantly to the iron hook in my skull upon
which I am hung, that is, my destiny was concrete—and seltzer!
Rot breaking out like giggles in casket drill, and all because
of this rockwall which certainly had not prepared itself for the
drenched stumblers who were to find no entrance,
    thus blessed imagination creates exit, each puddle depres-
sion gets in tow, all nature has arrived and is bridal,
    I am affirmed
    which beats my affirming nature
    only barely,

a rockwall cares its way in, the crystal of vision leads out,
like a panopticon, through mazes of disappearing nibbles,

and one who once waited for his fontanel to close over,
stretches in mind in Minotaur embrace.

THE HORIZON THAT DOESN'T GO AWAY

Wind in the chestnuts.
About-to-burst fuzz-prickly pods.
Artaud snapping in electro-shock,
as if to *shit* blood through his navel
he had to be roasted open.

Who isn't in therapy with Death,
Persephone the handmaiden?

Who isn't decorated with all
he's squeezed through
his rusty, rock accordion?

As we return upon ourselves,
the erasures bear strange babies.
The traces seem fugal, foetal weavings
Giacometti-wrapped in restarts and retreats.

Does the writing wear a groove
capable of rinding first mind?

For that seems my task, to burst pod
and find myself in the cave of head,
where inside ceased to be aside
and took on the grandeur of:
rock is continuation,
on it I'll boat my finger.

Skull is cave once the brain is eaten.
Man is skull once the cave is abandoned.

124

What was eaten in Lascaux?
No—what *was* Lascaux is now eaten.
As if the first bull were not yet consumed,
as if the wall's will read:
before you are entitled to my wealth,
you must eat all my corpses.

[Les Bois d'Envaux]

CONVERSATION PIECE

Pardon me, Robert Browning, for some time I've wanted to dump your Duchess out the window and install, as a new conversation piece, the European cattle complex,
the filthy Satan into whose sirloin we seem to be forever cutting,
perched on tombstones, wrapped in togas, doggedly consuming the dead ancestor as the condition for receiving inheritance,
as if the earth itself were a horned god to be devoured,
a diabolic version of mother (it's breast envy, you bastards), in whom we might lay to rest once and for all this unwinable argument of spirit vs matter, and from whom we might innocently be reborn!

This conversation piece has fangs protruding from its foot,
its steer-like leg is of a milky marble so elegant as to recall the Fertile Crescent,
the thigh, bulbous and lean, reflects our heel as it arches and defines the lower body ark,
or pelvic bowl, over whose rim drape fauna heads, like exhausted electric parts—
viewed from above, it is a tiny isle, with miniature Chinese bridges leading to a moat of blood, inside which bull Adam and heifer Eve hump entranced before a writhing *chef d'orchestre.*

[Salina]

THE NOT-SO-MYSTERIOUS KOAN

I chanced upon my primal home
—division. The Great Mother and God
laid out, side by side.
Nearby, the slaughterbench
oozed a little Ganges from each chop.

Her vulva, hacked with rot,
formed: "What now is the sound
          of one tree falling?"
There was a scent of blackboard
filled with chalk zeros. In this urn field,
my mind became a ball court,
                    the leaf glitter
the sparking milling of cuneiforms.
Bereft of my double indemnity,
I watched the wedge-shapes form
                    a doughnut of light
against whose cenote-black center
I pressed my male, or right, hand, leaving,
as a negative, the outline of Hispaniola,
                    My Lai.

And God? looking like a Frankenstückling
scythed from the sky tit,
one earthwormy knucklebunch
clutched a wadded scrap:

"Kafka's ax, rotating in outer space."

OUT OF THE KAT GODEU

[for Jerome Rothenberg's
60th birthday]

Before I was free I was multiform
I was a sharp damascened sword
Drops of water in the upper air   The most ardent star
The beginning of the ancient word
Before I was Jerome I was Rothenberg
Before Rothenberg I was Red Mountain
I was Navaho I was Seneca
Bubbles in beer   Honey milk and soap
A harp string transformed 9 years into foam
A witness among killing center stones

It is not I who will not sing
I sing powerfully if obscurely
I enter *the scaled beast* bearing 6 million *heads*
A hard fight it is for the man on the mat
Annihilation is every field, the sound of any train
"Shoah." A backyard in Encinitas CA
coextensive with Buenos Aires, Treblinka
"There is no place that does not see you.
~~You must change your life~~."

Peeled of eternity—the riddled self,
                              crouched.
On Leon Golub's limpwristed leg-armed
canine, a military head, flummoxed,
   lit by interior gangrene.
Have you just grasped, Blue Sphinx,

what man has done with the animal powers
  by which he entered time?

    *

    The delicate crystal before its candle
      holds arsenic gold,
    the stone of the apricot comingling
      with the eau-de-vie.

As for the Budapest Hilton spiders,
they work in huge, filth-furred webs, outside
  the 17th floor restaurant.
We were seated by the picture window—there they were,
  the dinner entertainment!
"To eat living creatures on a plate-glass plate,
to do it vertically high in the sky
while you humans purr over disguised steer.
Here we work in night and fog, boring into whatever
  earth coughs up,
steaming up moth news, handcuffed to
  our unpruned jaws."

    *

The young Soviet soldier at the side of the road standing by
the raised barrier as we drove past had a skinned, unborn,
lumber-hewn face. Something stuck in a uniform and left in
the rain. "They're sent abroad at 18 for 3 or 4 years," Gyula
Kodolanyi says, "hated by the foreign population, lackeys of
officers, no women." I try to summon the face of the one we
passed at the edge of the woods, and draw forth Soutine ghosts,
butchered meat, the sweetness of youth cankered, remote. What
did we look like to him?

    *

North of Gyor
7 cracked concrete doors
  commemorate, with cobalt-blue interstices,

129

Miklos Radnoti's etched words:
"I lived in an age so ugly, men killed
not only on command, but for pleasure."

Radnoti, Rothenberg and I live in a country
where men, who cut the vaginas out of My Lai women,
    walk free.

Across the road from the monument, a marsh.
Mossy blue willows twist from the mass grave
    which, in 1943,
included Radnoti and, in his overcoat pocket,
    his last hexameters.

                    *

                            It is the
        injured toughness of what is used
moves me.
                    Under Tibor's scraggly cherry trees,
the blue, rubble-soft bench used to be a door.
I instantly loved its blister hives.
Is this love facing the bomb? Not to be
                            prehistoric,
    but to have something in
        one's character   grandfather
an older world   in crumble suspension
                            here.

        *

Over Lake Balaton this evening, lightning,
sudden floods of violet squid . . .

All of Hungary faces Balaton,   root lake,
entrance to the Magyar underworld.
Here, Sandor Ferenczi is still slithering in and out
    of mother sound,
he waves farewell to his sperm as it alone

disappears into her bio-folds to reach,
he believes, at last, Thalassa!
The Hungarian longing for suicide, the no-sea ache.

Balaton, reticule, in which eyes
            of the ancient marsh
        still glint with lavender nights.
I say it with North American optimism,
which carries such nuclear embarrassment
            in its hold.

Ferenczi continues to yearn for a journey
    on an animal of water.
It bears him on and on, he cannot tell its size,
    or where its head begins—
        but he is moving on its rolling
                aquaflesh,
there are thousands of cherry-red
                gashes in its sides,
    he tastes the sweet syrup of one,
and then another, and the feel
of Last Supper is living
                infant on his tongue . . .

[1986–1992]

HARDBALL

I see the raped and beaten black body
I say I see the raped and beaten black body
I say I a white man see the raped and beaten black body,
for the next 39 lines you will hear Rodney beaten,
for they swingled him, they
buttfucked his eyes, they crosslabored him,
they kicked mocked and backed him, backed
him good, they sought to south him, to speedball
him north, then they toed his cream, they stepped
balled him, they whitemen outvoted his groin,
then they went for his teeth, he tried to scream they
        mouthstick
fucked him, they kickass arabed him—did they Baghdad
        him?
Did they 170,000 Iraqi children him?

Did they sewage water system him?

Did they Kurd and carpet bomb his retreat?

And in case you think I'm mixing oil with macadam,
they beat Rodney King as if he were wood
or cockroach, both cock and rock,
they beat him because he was black nearly dead man,
cause he was nigger,
now all you white students repeat   with   me
you who never will   you who have no moral will   Did
they beat him as your dad might've beat your mom?
Because women and blacks are the beatabilities,

132

kill this black white woman because heshe is,

kill this living black white pink and blue trunk

kill this human trunk that bulges and weeps.
Beat what I am,   beat what you are,
beat to the beat,   but no masturbation is strong enough
to rip out the white, to push it up, calcite,
huge chalk tunnels of your come in you,
to so dispossess us of the human that we must regard
    our birth channel
forever in challenge with us?   Aie, we are, in birth,
and we are beating our birth,   we are,   in birth,
beat Rodney   beat the earth
and know now   beat the earth is no longer
    dance step or game title
but swerve to piles in the watcher's eyes
while the dead pile up under,
    the dead, the beavers and
    all those fleas we never wanted to name.

VARIATION ON A LINE BY POUND

"The humane man has amity with the hills"
the main hue is an amity in the hills
the human hue is an am, an I am of the hills
an am I am, to be haunted always by
am I of the hills and to keep in amity
in spite of the humane, the human amity
that as an I am would replace the hills.
   All these hues are so much
has with the hills, their having is
without amity, amless hills
                onto which
man projects amity.
The humane man projects and sees through amity,
his amity is hued, hewn, so much hooha—
   to be nitty with the hills?
Hills infest the humane man with what he is,
a hill hue, a who of amless hill.

Words that are not in any sentence paw
as if to break down fragile amity.

The humane man has amity with the hills
for his amlessness depends, as well as his am,
thus does the hill man have amity
   with what is humane.
One might call oneself Hillman
to offer amity the mane of hill.

134

GROUND

Is it possible that language wears through, wears through itself, becomes, as this path, a thing rubbed out?

All paths are scuffed, as are words, all paths look done in.

The nature of the path: to be worn into. No indication ever of how many passed.

Dirt, chaos bone, metaphor-barren stones that imply an arbitrary gist.

Once, as if in birth, something pushed through high grass, a family? a string of goats?

Anonymity is the most known force.

At the heart of every specific direction, a characterless path.

Sentences reused become pebbled voids, comforting to the mouth, yet of a deadness so obdurate poetry to be fresh must crack them open.

We pass so thoroughly over, our going sounds self-dismissal as our eyes clamp, or clomp against, destination's nearest rung.

No scene is ever reseen.

Each time is new.

My voice, wording its way while traveling unlimited narrowing, lacks and is.

Lacks an is.

All, under leveling sea winds, gesticulates
asway.

[Ile de Ré]

ON SUNLIT GARAGE FRONT
fluttermounting pigeon shadows
and in the shadows
        female outlines,
La Roche-de-Lalinde, 11,000 BCE.

        Most ancient women,
            the egg still to be laid
gripped in their protruding butts.

COOKING

I slide down like a fireman into a cauldron-shaped machine.
                    The discourse
                 shifts, scaly zucchini
wants to be scrubbed. Mother said: get outta the tub
soon as you finish washing,
so I scrub and consider the chicken, the cold
under her arms as I carried her into the hospital toilet.
All of life is present every moment.
We know this, or I do, dimly,
I wipe up something from the chopping block, it tastes
like 16th Street—best I can do,
       my birth? The flecks are more precious than
weight of bird in hand. Open the wine.
Curious, the antagonism wafting from the just-pulled.
But who wants to be opened? Down in the blood force,
I dream while I cook. Dreaming is
a kind of cooking, body between waffle irons bed and
       night,
ghosts of the introjected sipping and picking.
I am closer to Caryl in bed
than at table, but tapers shadow us here.
Are we re-enacting the primal snack
as we cut, munch, and talk? The tall sip of Chinon
that plunges to my belly,
a shore bird zapping up a crab?
Have you looked into your mouth,
considered the Labrador of ice floes, jungular lagoons,
infintestinal havens under invasion
as the tongue, trapped rhino, goes through its
       plungings, so articulate

after 20,000 years,   then Andrei Codrescu on NPR:
he too hates David Duke—I throw in more Louisiana,
cleaning a shrimp: serrated knife down the back
held against the chopping block edge,
swole gut tract furls back, husk won't disposal, so
I bag'm, thoroughly rinsing the headless, footless
     Paleo bodies under harsh cold,
each point of cooking so interesting,
                    I know you appreciate it
having shopped so carefully for all I fondle.
To clean a squid is to have a hand up the goddess.
To do so makes me want to help a cow give birth.
To cook makes me want to disembowel myself and eat.
Cooking is a form of labyrinthine pacing,
and is without fear, until we make contact with
the soul of the beloved, for whom we cook.
Then the two of us are out on plates
looking up into this gorgeous autumn. We are old,
and sliding about, but the dry golden trash
     still clinging to the maples
is a kind of funky Greek Keatsean urn.

Kenneth Burke, 94, is happy for a tasty meal.
He has a chic grey cap, and settles in
at our table on his pillowed chair.
Salmon without oil, or salt,
spinach, rice, Pilsner Urquell.
He said that night: "Beauty is Truth, Truth Beauty—
     Body is Turd, Turd Body"   and giggled.

Each evening we sit down to these bodies
     in cocoon, these woven green beans,
this artichoke harboring so many compressed
thorny lips. A delicate char molded by
     the coldest lake depths,
parts of my mother, parts of our mothers' mothers,
     myself, yourself.
               The wind rises outside,

138

the gold, rouge-red, orange bonfired leaves are down.
We are skeletons eating amongst skeletons.
                                        This
      is the delicious thrust and realization.

THE WINE GRAVEYARD

It is raining quietly on the wine graveyard tonight.
Through amber, bacchic curves, runny cobwebs,
reveries and revels mingle. Here the poorest and
                        most opulent are lees,
inky lakes, combs of whitening mold, purples whose
cranial murmurs Baudelaire might have heard,
witnesses to our need to pull the blinds at twilight,
illuminate the dining room as if it were a womb,
                        and we, the living,
able to cross the bridge of a sip into that shallow well
where memory is abyss and the phantoms rising,
the friendly shapes of a dissolution to be embraced—

for the mind is the poor rained-upon place,
bottleneck upon bottleneck tear into each.
We share the instruments in the symphony of the dead,
your kettle drum tonight is my fife tomorrow,
                        my glass this evening
your urn in a future so vast the bottles blur,
a magma that a toast might staunch, and so,
                        as we pour, against a flame
to tell us when clarity is invaded by flecks
that once contributed to our most burgundy premises,
we find ourselves between two intoxications—
the foetal binge in which mother's laughter sounded
                        like rumbling trucks,
and the other, this hive of blackened bottles.

Here we are truly put to bed, tucked in

sister to brother, baron to sutler, and the lips
that graze our foreheads, are they not,
as they purse, sipping, if only air,
our natal bouquet, our floridity, our devastation?

GUYTON PLACE

Is it our work to push doghouses, jeans
and waffle irons into earth's orifices,
to shun them as soon as we use them?
Isn't everything we shape imbued with what we can
    and cannot imagine?
Somehow, in Rilke's time, things shined, were company.
            Wine, shaped by the vintner,
"the savor of the earth, made intelligible to man."
In 1925, Rilke wrote: "Now, from America, empty indifferent
things are pouring across, sham things, *dummy* life . . . A house,
in the American sense, an American apple or a grapevine over
there, has *nothing* to do with the house, the fruit, the grape into
which went the hopes and reflections of our forefathers . . . Live
things, things lived and conscient of us, are running out and can
no longer be replaced. *We are perhaps the last still to have known
such things.*"

Update: in the core of America, as if at a hearth pit,
whose tentacles spread throughout the body politic:
Reagan's face, a mosaic composed of contra-
Midas touches, disposables, things adults no longer love
reproduced in miniature for their children,
life a non-sequitor. A Salvadoran woman returns home,
to find her family's heads set on the set table's
    dinner plates.
The Reagan face, frozen in vomit-guffaw.
Imagine seeing his stomach!
                    Take the Mount Elliott Exit
off I-94 south via the old Detroit "Black Bottom"
    to Heidelberg, and turn right.

Tyree Guyton's *Funhouse* is on the left.
It seems to cook there, in snow or summer,
                    "belly of the shark,"
panopticon of American childhood and poverty.
African-American childhood, African-American poverty.
"Perhaps we are *here* in order to say: house, bridge, well,
gate, jug, fruit tree, window—at most: column, tower . . ."
But, collapsed wheel chair? Plastic yellow horseshoe?
Squashed truck tire with "cookie monster" peeking out?
Perhaps Rilke's "lovers" could merely pronounce such
    words, in the aristocratic world of Muzot.
                                On Heidelberg,
the street-abandoned is returned to the sides, roofs, porches,
    front yards and sidewalks of 2 houses.
Imagine "Blue Poles" tied around a house so staggered
    it can barely sustain structure,
"drippings" 1 to 5 layers deep, no longer "paint"
but a rubble ropology of bedsprings nailed over window,
jammed in crutches, one with LA Gear basketball shoe,
porkpie hat forced into white telephone receiver,
                            grey underpants,
tricycle poked window,   brooms through springs

fireman boot snaking eaves gutter

baby doll heel draped wire mesh

hammock loaded kitchen counter, to which nailed
                            saddle oxford,
hunk of grey shag carpet slapdashed white,
hobbyhorse (no front hoofs), peach mattress,
lawnmower blades, friction tape winding
                            industrial ducts,
rusted wheelbarrow pan, blue bath towel
                            stained scarlet,
water heater (sorrel around its tilted base)

on front porch:
empty-overnight-case-piled phone booth

TV innards skewered plastic tenpin

TONKA Turbo-Diesel toy
rusted car frame
baby-blue scooter
smashed mannequin head on prong

hobbyhorse hoofs gripping sagging eaves gutter
(what do thy eyes see upside down?)
beret on toilet plunger,   rusted tin world globe

"fence"
of semi-submerged
semi tires
M. Amelia
wife of Geo Zahn
& daughter of
Chas & Anna Bleicher
Born Nov 8 1854
Died Dec 7 1877
rusted-apart lunch box, Suzie Homemaker stove,
motorcycle spray-graffitied chartreuse, footstool,
oil landscape by R. Robinson, catcher's mask,
half a license plate [MR 6
toilet bowl, its contents: "Jack Lemmon" Weekender hat,
purple leather high heel pump

Abortion
is
Murder
vote NO [X]
on B
be the voice of the
UNBORN

144

(4 blocks away, Tyree's friend, "the junkman,"
lives in a wheelless school bus surrounded by *ruined* junk.
In his pot-bellied stove, behind the driver's seat,
    he burns spars from torched houses.
At 77, he seems wired with energy, lives on Wild Irish
    Rose,
a man alive in his own graveyard. One frosty December,
we all walked the ice-rutted alley while he yelled
"I'MA **SCIENTIST** MOTHERFUCKIN COON!")

Malte Laurids Brigge: "and the fusel ordor of sweltering
feet . . . tang of urine and the burn of soot and the grey
    reek
of potatoes, the heavy, smooth stench of aging grease."
These sensations we must imagine here—
line upon line of watermarks, chains of object scum,
                    haphazard, intricate.

A block away, "the whorehouse,"   3121 Mount Elliott:
nailed-up naked baby doll parts,
                    the unconceived
washed out by sink-top douche? Doll head
                    lobotomized on porch rail,
rotted blue rubber dildo,   diapered torso roast.

Next door, Tyree's grandpa, Sam Mackey, 92,
sits at the kitchen table, drawing with crayons
versions of the androgyne. "In that distant chamber,
a bearded queen, wicked in her dead light,"
old Wallace Stevens wrote. Grandpa Mackey's have
    arm-like tits, gigantic dicks.

How paradise might look to the cast-out serpent
                    raising its head
to look back on the emptied place of origin.
All once inside now nailed to Eden's outer wall
                    —and the Cherub?

Nailed to the top of the wall, strutting,
as if to Sousa. The dream detonated,
all things in Babel on earth's multifoliate
                              cross.

                                        [1989]

DEBRIS

It was crucial to see that my face in water
an image of my face
is neither mother nor father
but a shadow into whose interior
fish can pass, investing Narcissus
with passing otherness
as this phantom ripples apart.

If I am hooped over history, a mockery of Nut,
it is because, with my fingers in Lascaux,
and my toes scraping the present,
I have sought unbearable images for an age
whose concreteness is mixed with those
who were commanded from the ramps.

I work with the debris of Lascaux
in which the manganese is a kind of bran,
through which the radiance
from no attached placenta
ripples out, a bandsaw rainbow,
whose center stripe
is turtles
all the   Every instant of October
way d   would yield an epic.
    ow   Is this why we overwhelm ourselves?
      n   To ask for all here now
                is to beckon
                the back of the abyss
                forward, to feel it in our

bowl of cereal,
the under all
on the move.

    *

Primo Levi, you worker of a nothingness so
hesitatingly received by imagination—
your body rises, the modest sun rifting late
  Michigan autumn.
You were right to complete your abyss,
to etch in fat
the way of ashes.

    *

How in March, I regard April, May . . .

  but how tonight
  stirring the rabbit compote,
    as if back in Kyoto, 26 years ago,
    the Ibuki kitchen, alone with tea,
  each detail blazed,
  was artery, each
  lace of vein

nailed me to my blazon.

    *

Once I had a son. His name was Salamander,
and he disappeared in New York City
in a schoolroom haunted by Reich's genital poetry
        burned on Gansevoort Pier.
A son, once, was there ever a once?
A son sounding my interior son, a male of my femaleness,
a boy who disappeared in my desertion,
the mirage of myself, a visitor
        with my own webbed eyes.
Once I had a son. His name was Filibuster,

148

and he disappeared in Cincinnati,
rummaging through his veins, seeking to cut
        in the instant of tying up,
dismissing the strength of the crocodile
for the titbits to be picked from its teeth.
Whose name was Salamander Filibuster,
who dallied in his pyre, a little kid,
                            a whittled id,
a boy naked and skinned, exhibited
    broken off from the rest of the ship,
a son, a figurehead, adrift in the shoals of America,
pressing a mushroom to his breast,
        adrift, a thin blue-veined mushroom
            to his white black-veined breast!

    *

    In Dave McKenna's back
    I watch my mother a young woman stretch

    the shadow play
    tall black-socked
    ankles tapping

    a cat so romantic my mother
    swims in his serge
    "O Clayton, it is tired here,
    lodged spinally
    who can rest?

    He don't look like much
    but once he takes off
    he covers more graveyard per chorus
    than you can shake a stick at!

    I'm happy inside McKenna's body,
    why at full tilt, he's my spectre!
    And you people think *artists are alive.*

When his fingers prey,
my guts become a prayer,
he's schmaltzy,
but that chicken fat is in there
'cause gals like gasoline
inflame his north!"

*

Pumpkin-colored spider
big as an oyster
—was mother ever mother?
Or is "she" this boiling of the soul
to combustionate its origin? To combustionate itself?
The soul eats from its own primal scene,
delights in rocks,
as Iguana, it mouths the head of Turtle,
upon whose Shell it is flexed.
"Behold Behemoth
the pact I have made with Thee"
In 7 League Boots,
Mother now appears, Her slavering Wolf face
crawled by Mice of the invisible,
Falcons pick moss from her jowls,
they collect Rabbits and Toads lost in the liquid
ebony of Her stare—
they bear us, as we bear ourselves, hatching
Scorpions at birth loaded, like aircraft carriers,
with babies.
I am in Her and She is alive.
I curl within Her parenthesis,
held by Her hearth life,
dipped in liquid gold.

POSITION PAPER

_____

It is always daybreak,
an octopus with golden eyes.
You stand not on zero
but on the zerocity of being.

The lifewire is looped between desire
        and fulfillment here,
imperfect adumbration of day
        breaking below.

From dragon jaws yawning
the hero is born to be beheaded
                by an elder.
The elder's problem:
he had a father. Be father free. Be
        daybreak. Wear this fissure
as Ptah wears falcon,
as an Aztec eagle warrior
looks out an open eagle beak.

I is not an other.
I is, in other. Rimbaud,
            you erred!
You took off your caul bonnet,
you thought you could go it alone.

The man enchased in daybreak
is the sunyata in his parents' gyre. Being
        runs clear, remains

unclear. Be verb, for they are ob-
    and subject,
   the frame
    you mirror.

MEXICO, 1959

Other who bears me, shoulders upon which
I have ridden ever since I learned to walk . . .

take me once more around the Chapala cantina.
Show me the pig head for pozole,
the beef carcass with its black overcoat of flies,
the faces of those warped by being,
                    not protected by having,
the drunken leer, the shawl-enmassed tableau,
the wounded man who invites me to share his cot,
whose side turns into a red lake when I am
                    spoonwise beside him . . .

bear me down through this lake,
help me respect the fiery sores of a cosmos
                    at one with its dimming.

Bear me through my background, the blocks of I.C.E.
Sparky's gelid yelping. Indiana from the height
                    of visionary stilts.
Behind the furnace the beating spot.
The beating-off spot. Lathe and coal bin. The vise.
Supplies of nails, Petty Girls, chisels.
Under 4705, Collodi. Wondrous workshop where the boy
                    was framed.

I was washed onto the rock of Vallejo
which had shot up through the waves,
had added selves to itself, a stalagmite
                    purifying its own moisture,

rock of water in sea of blood.
As a novice, I lived there,
farmed the stone, erected my shack.

Why must we infuse the rocks with color
                    beyond their granite
or scrape our hearts on maternal padlock?

Entrance is holy and is everywhere hidden.

Image is reality in the invisible world.

A dragon is a wisp of abyss bursting into bloom.

Wagon-wheeling clouds, the joy in Pinocchio's heart.

Metaphor, the single great gift, the bounce in the ride.

Everything is in potential regeneration,
                    underlined with terra
one apocope away from terror.

We the so-called living—aren't we only riders
        without a direction of our own?
Or in choosing our ghosts, through trusting them,
might we, voice to void, direct their roaming?

GORGEOUS GEORGE COMES POUNDING
DOWN THE BEACH

—————————————————————————————————

On the San Diego Freeway
    rising toward Mulholland—
azure ghosts of canyons,
        cobalt lime dusk.
Agnostic snarl of art, aerobics, pizza,
valet parking for Trashy Lingerie.
Sun tinsel streaming in 5 PM light so strong,
my eyes close driving, open to helicopters
walking the backyard on stalks of light.
Bricolage of tar Maya movie plaster.
"HI, my name's Bruce, I'm your waiter,
    I tried to kill myself last night."
Gladiator bright, collapsable city.
The Rolfed young man cries I am,
not realizing *I am* does not see.
So I'm 13, in my Aunt Georgia's trailer,
off Mulholland. I've been parked here
    while the adults play Canasta.
Stretched out on the bunk bed,
                turn on the tiny TV:
Gorgeous George comes pounding down the beach,
platinum locks atoss, bikinied,
    as if strolling the infinite.
Nature's radiation appears
        an angel layered in coke
stretched out on sushi cooler ice,
    Goddess Ikatakomagurouni.
LAX landing flights flashing hero no one
    while up the Strip I chug

below the toe level of billboard gods,
oily, puffed up in platinum heels.
Jackie Collins' anima-black mane,
                    neon lips,
"exquisitely jacketed in depths of anthracite."
Madonna, "The Frida Kahlo Story,"
                    laquered red nails,
silky hair crisscrossed in meticulous
    braids—visited by the Rockefellers,
        her unhealable abdominal wound.
Perhaps Frida is LA's patron saint?

On Melrose, mascaraed punk mannequins
    are digging "Day of the Dead." La Muerte:
        the exfoliating skull sending north
                    Mexican macabre gaiety,
dens that abutt globally:
the cleaning woman's husband
                    decapitated in Guatemala
appears on TV.
                    Kali-fornia face,
    Kali's fornix, Marilyn's whee!
her sagging frontier bodice line
where men are at once larvae and Valentino.
Brittle chrome candy of this Western edge,
haunted not as Brittany by "finisterre"
    (thus world-end everywhere)
but by the American Icarus dream: "Mounting
upon the wings of light into the Great Expanse"
Gorgeous George comes pounding up the beach.
Hockney-sketchy immortality
                    swimming pool deep,
a water blue sky in whose bowl
I too steer, emperiled by cancerous fish,
a human being looking like a scuba effete
wandering unpeopled streets, wearing
                    my house on my head,
my possessions pyramiding my sides

156

a mobilary Mesoamerican relief.
                    Porky and Bugs
come tumbling through the palms,
squirting my sunglasses with hot-dog
                    shaped diners
and saber-tooth perfume!

NAVEL OF THE MOON

The man who is always wanting to see
now knew he must imbibe semen,
    but in imagination—
as at the openings of the mountainous mother
he had perceived the stones were so alive
they were freezing. He had to release
the semen parachute way too long nailed to
the zenith of male brain,
had to let it pass through his eyes
to experience the octopodal
sensation of submarine drapery,
to be thin as a veil, but also to fit into
the carapace of a crab. The project, then,
is to let the treasure descend
through the interior zoo of chakras
until Kundalini, blind as Tiresias,
coiled so long her rattles have gone soft,
raises her head and gulps the displaced jade
—not nag, nor strumpet,
but the nearly untranslatable fool's gold,
the glacial division in muelos-elevated man.

It is time to be tender to stone,
to see it as semen, as the finite of the inside
Big Hole Woman scratched animals into.
Or are we all animals of snow,
composed of the avalanche of mother's milk,
through which flows a warm but alpine stream?
How you'd love to believe its source is in your head,
maggot in a uniform of buttoned gold!

Autumn, you lie least. As the harvest
swings into full view, the cornucopia tightens.
Could I but interrupt mother and father
for only a moment, would I,
in the sensorium of that smoking lubricity,
inhale a contradiction so total
that, when they started up again,
I would be their rhythm?

Mother, can't you see I'm a root borer?
I'm reholing the word that was your breast.
Stand back, ego, shrink to
the immensity of the nipple absence
over which your paradise is stretched.
The soul, most honorable cannibal,
lined with the mead of its oldest kill,
        its blindness.

Caryl's hand touching
went through my thigh at the rush of love,
which is liquid, relentlessly sweet,
muscle seltzer—but it did not go completely through,
it is suspended,
        she is suspended,
        her hand in my thigh, calming,
how much she calms
        in suspension there.

At Monte Alban, before a *danzante*,
the shadow of Ana Mendieta bends.
A flattened man all surface like Ana,
cheek of stone, a lily-groined hunchback,
pages of a scattered stone book,
dismembered at the core of vision,
three halves that never join,
two orgasms jolting past each other.
Thus compassion. Thus tenderness mixed with gravel.
In the tip of the solar arrow,

I discover my mother tied and splayed.
A great snail has arrived in the plaza.
We cry Beached Whale!
In metaphor, the primal anxiety:
everything is nothing
something is a toadstool under which
ragged elves are cowering.
How long does it take to get the weight of the earth
    through my head?

        Coatlicue leans forward
just enough to offer a worm shade.
Before Her as a man, I felt my infant size
before my mother—or let's say
Coatlicue is the size surrounding the hole
I made in mother's apple—and so, indeed,
I am a worm in the shade Serpent Skirt offers
—with whom one never shakes hands.
One shakes *hearts* with Coatlicue,
for she too is part of the cornucopia,
part of the great snail's retinue.
All true answers are questioned
by the 2 rattlesnakes that like facing
question marks fuse as Her head.

        Bitter river
poets would say flows into the metaphor-
confabulated split tongue whose root is lost
in Coatlicue's cistern breast,
tongue waving from a peculiar mound—listen:
as if a century plant attempted to free itself,
having blossomed, or, have you blossomed?
Was birth that good? Mother's apple that rich?
Isn't your heart always that apple,
pumping serpent, caduceus tree rooted
lower body, her feline hindquarters,
the aroma of her menstrual pool
out of which fairies first flitted?

160

As I stared at my stool,
the faint blue forms of mountains,
a fat crimson worm entered the mountain,
a male worm wearing a menstrual shawl—then blank,
nothing but milk delivery, the gangue of myth . . .

Against the underlight of Oaxaca
the night sky in suspended rise,
the necropolis in suspended fall.
We are nestled, forever, as now, or never,
in soft bone arms, buttressed by breeze and the wail
from the zenith tube into which liquid night flows,
a kind of larval ebony for ballplayer's hands,
the braid of events in the fleeing stream,
the present the parachute's weighted pouch,
the past its cape, the future
the rising hidden smile of the ground.
The firmest, most loosened poem meets us
with the force of
am I vain to hold my report open
while being written, so that we know
no more than a given instant realizes
—realizes? makes real, like makes water,
meaning re-leases loss, showing blocks,
the block is seen through
but only as a winding window at the mercy of
I stand in a rushing tower and write
with fluid pen on a tablet with a blank of its own—
what I remember are only my experiences.
The power of time, wider and deeper than life,
hurtles around skullracks, boulders with no recall,
body crates in which the gagging
if divine marrow is experienced on a plane
I know of but do not know.
Flower is consumed lmost faste th n ap ears
then *and*, dear procrastination, seeks to add
and my tablet gratefully sucks in my pen.

Time is layered. Each beginning deepens
as if each leaf weighed its tree,
and thus where I stand: the weight of me?
Infant pulled through the thighs of earth,
infant emerging from the crotch of stone,
or is it stone emerging from man,
what is hardest in man, the bearing of non-being,
to be a finite cul-de-sac
impacted with seminal angel.

I am pinned against the base of the Southern Cross
to a position, a vane over
the tumulus of my hopeless central sleep,
here with my pots and dolls,
buried alive in my background,
in the crested fist of the specificities
I've been hung with, have chosen to wear.
The white Western heterosexual moves
no revolutionary boulders. Unlike the Césaire-man,
he does not speak for the poor.
Even if he is not to be zapped,
but his boll weevils spun into porridge,
he is still a mink in the flavor—
    something that won't go down,
  or that does,
    failing those stacked
      in the flues.

"navel of the moon" Mexico
first disinterred me, a black cape of flies
took off from the pineapple of my innocent heart.
This is where I'll bury my poetry,
blood gate of the moon, vale whose path
is the backs of ants, glossy
scarlet road, conveyor mirror,
this is where I always wanted to play,
aloft, on penile dream stilts,
a Gulliver-man, in collage with time.

162

I am the man who waded in man,
who ate man's marrow and report it is without source.
WOT TIS SOR ROW the Noh ghost intoned.
"dirty water which nevertheless cleans a pail"
the menstruating dreamer replied.
I, Aerial, spat between the two,
I, Aerial, freed by the two,
saw a girl dying in bed, her hand a rose tree,
crawled in with her, let self
form a moat around her, a halo,
then the tree bloomed a fairy shower,
each wore a tiny fig pinafore,
each carried a sparkler as she circumambulated the tree.
"We come in self-annihilation and the grandeur of
        inspiration—
take the foul deposit in the cooking pot
and preserve it, for it is the source of heartage.
Come with us under this red rock,
we will show you the beast Blood Girl rides,
her broom bull, cratered, incandescent,
whose sides are open portals to the black manta shadow
on which we dreamers ebb and flow."

And we were followed into Monte Alban
by a little mongrel bitch
still nursing her litter,
our consort on that moonless night.
She rested by us as we sat, filthy, frisky,
wagging to the parking lot
where I wanted to adopt her.
Literal man, you've been adopted,
sick little dog, little Shulamite on the sward—
on her leash, power flows into your throat.
The work is everlasting conversion,
the mother is endless, the work is
everlasting conversion. Merton is electrocuted,
Vallejo's death curls a scorpion mark,
Caravaggio under a nitroglycerin sun

copulates with his own wounds.
Against vampiric literalism, hold the metaphor,
burn the cross with mental pain,
it will spring forth again, a violet,
a summer storm, the bellows tear,
the cinder burns through one's palm.
Today I have made contact with
the immortality of error. Alchuringa,
impinge! Open your foramen magnum to me.
Between genitals and the brain
there are only exploded bridges.

                              [Mexico City/Oaxaca,
                              May/June, 1991]

164

CEMPASUCHIL

       Odysseus' *ofrenda*
was a ewe-blood-filled trench.
He went down to the realm of souls—
we today anticipate their visit here.
They inhale the food we set out for them
then depart, without conversation.
      At 600 BCE, the distance
between the living and the dead was shorter,
Odysseus *spoke* with Tiresias,
received prophecy, mind penetrated mind.
The tree growing out La Mano Magica's patio wall
bears cactus pads to Oaxaca's October 30 sky,
but our dead are inaudible,
invisible, —is it because we
    expect them to come to
us? and when they do, are they so
weary no sacrifice can enable them
    to speak?

      In *The Wasteland*
Eliot set out food in tins,
Tiresias, the double-sexed one,
   was the middle wall
through which events transpired.
If I ask who are my dead?   [October 31]
Christobal Colón appears,
    a vast scorpion
whose back is littered with
   70 million corpses,
      he is punching

165

the smallpox cash register,
        arms pop up, legs,
a Spaniard sharpens his sword on the eyeball
            of a continent.
On each side of the slit,
unknown species grow like hair,
tapir and cherimoya, the anaconda, the llama,
I dwell in this image,
            the sword
sharpened on off shore whetstones,.
working against the eyeball of a continent
as species ooze, or fur, on either side,
as it slices in and in,

        Amamatando   [Museo Tamayo,
    whose mouth   November 1]
is not puckered to forever-receding
    breasts?
The Olmecs knew the wisest man
is the largest infant, that inscape
is no escape, is natal, is a rain-
    forest of virus and need,
bald, I am howling for milk,
asleep, sitting up drunk in
this frightening coffin with tits,
and very happy to be stretched here.
        Chambi saw   [Martín Chambi, *Museo*
the rictus and the reception, warm   *de Arte Contemporaneo*
    human welcome of a man   *de Oaxaca*, Inauguración
on his own picked potato pile,   30 de octubre de 1992]
while his other flashes daft
    at the peak of the heap,
one-sandaled man, aggressive with fiddle,
who isn't ready to play?
who isn't waiting for chicha?
        under a dusty hatband
in the 100° shade, on dirt,
a crosslegged infant adult, holding out my cup,

who doesn't shake his rattle before
                any passerby?
who isn't waiting for Columbus
    as the scarlet standards of
            Santo Domingo
waggle by,   sails without ships,
the Pinta before every cathedral
                door?

I am Nayarit, blind, with fingers
        at the end of my flippers,
shoulders poxed, with only a stiff napkin
                across my knees,
my breasts tattooed targets,
my toes protruding from my knees,
I know that in holy imagination
        all is in recombination,
I know that I am pregnant
my navel a hub,
            in diaper-bib,
elephant-eared,
        giggling milk spurts,
I am so wise mush is leaking from
                my mouth,
come into my stomach hole,
imagine the contents of this
                cylindrical dark.
Here the brothel has dried,
the lunch stand, here a quail in galoshes
is kicking the bundle of bones
Quetzalcoatl dropped on his
        journey out of Mictlan,
    hollow lower body, source
& synthesis of Hell, icebox of embers,
            where a bent aged
grasshopper broods on human fate—
freckled, with doodads
        clustering its ears,

aged warrior awaiting rebirth,
   sneezing, while drivel
turns back, miraculous curare,
   the blood that fears blood.
I crouch in Jaliscan time,
so grotesque as to be totally recognizable,
my begging bowl stacked with Coca Cola bottles,
a lewd photo of JC Oates
   in my watch pocket,
my snot freezes before my nose
   into snout protector,
now that my head is on inside out
I face the past, the future
                  behind,
me, I skull the past, speaking
      in future behind,
I wear the lintel of the future
                  behind,
solemn, I am still too solemn,
what new green head is waiting
   to break through my skull?

———
———

In Atzompa cemetery I felt a ringing in my hands
as if they'd been asleep
   and circulation like racing sand,
cempasúchil scattered   [connec:
   drapes and rosaries of shredded   to Olson's
Day of the Dead flowers,   Black Gold
      "African Marigold,"   Flower?]
accompanied by magenta cockscomb,
   cresta de gallo, or pata de león,
dirt mounds, only a few with tombstones,
palm stalks stuck in the mounds,
            overarched by a 10-trunked
                  fig tree,

168

plain redug graveyard enlightened
   by petals the color of healthy
                  chicken skin.

Here Arnulfo Mendoza has tied 2   [Mary Jane & Arnulfo's
   packs of Fiesta cigarettes to   living room above
a full mescal bottle, one burning   La Mano Magica]
                  candle,
cempasúchil sprays, Day of the Dead
                  bread,
it's raining, the altar in the corner
   grows darker as I sit,
is his dad here now? He has a photo   [in which he is carrying
   to guide him and the adopted   a bottle of mescal
                  baby son   to which have been tied
whining in the bedroom.   2 packs of Fiestas]
            Outside the old wood door,
stained grey walls, a spill of magenta
                  bougainvilla.
A ceramic angel bears a basket between her wings
or is it a candlestick?
                  I'd like to identify
this darkened room and rain atmosphere,
it's shaped like Sunday in the American midwest—
as the raindrops crack, the marigold
                  odor wafts
a small white African-face mask,
      small shoulder bags,
a steer-horned devil mask, rugs to cushion
whoever's back presses against
   the long living room bench.
A mermaid with raspberry nipples and arabesque
"designer" tights over part of her fish portion
leaps, and draws a toothy fish toward her breasts—
will she nurse it? in Mexican male mind
a woman is nursing a non-human creature,
a little pig, or dog—Arnulfo's mermaid has wings,
long ropy brown hair. The sky resounds azure,

                                    169

scarlet, her tail is earth gleaming ivory
as she bursts her sea egg, and she also wears
a jeweled sombrero, or so I observe,
in respect for the otherness
        embreasted in
this room——
                        tomorrow it is Clinton vs Bush
        2000 miles away,
the dead now visiting will return to
                Mictlantecuhtli
as American voters argue
a man who might be honest vs a man
whose entire being exhales lies. O
dead, are you aware of our doings here?
Must we invent new sacrifice to sense
        the capstone of the soul?
Aren't we always in sacrifice
as the planet shifts its pox,
   Iraq yesterday, Somali today,
Bolivian mothers 10 deep in kids, dad face down
                smashed in road mud,
ghastly synthesis forever at work,
                sacrifice
and massacre to make us feel?
                        As if art eats this shit
to transform a bit of the cruelty
man and nature, like two jaws, provide,
        mouth eating its own teeth,
its tongue, self-devouring
                        yet feebly renewing life,
all things feel of skull if you touch them
                with respect,
and the one you love, not once does she
        deflect you from your task,
the musicians start up, rain drizzling
                into their tubes,
if she seems to divide you, Rilke,
   from your work, it only means

she mirrors your mortality so keenly
  you innerly divide and project
the conflict as love vs vision.
                              Or so
I'd be in the tearing of desires
the sound itself regarding its fray——

                I am whipped.   [Recalling
I sleep in reddened surf.   Elaine Morgan's
Earth bakes. My simian   "aquatic
                blood   hypothesis"]
mingled with menstrual blood.
What time is it? Miocene o'clock.
Under dream, there are toasters,
                a grillwork of
lactation, virus and bone. Under dream,
I cannot walk. Jellyfish pass.
On the beach, lions are building the
                first pylons,
or Babel. Gutteral lozenge in my
                broken mouth.
To incorporate, to sense *corps*
  in the most viscous word.
I am whipped, and pry into my
                lashwork.
Césaire is near now, a caramel shadow
whose fins touch my own . . .

        In and out, the miraculous
  slosh, the running in of surf, corpse
afloat, inlet. Caramel shadow,
shadow of Freud, of Lucifer,
tombstone-shaped man, man of phallic shoulders,
                woman with vulval head.
All parts may be exchanged,
the beauty, the horror of it! Idi
        Amin doll, voodoo

blond Christ, football crucifix,
the stadium a caldron with Lady Macbeth cheerleaders.
James Wright gallops past.
In and out, slimy dick, slimy cunt.
The strata of sex and language. All
    can be used. All
unlike a detergent, spins, washing the mind,
foul, fodder, the parental force in gnats,
the latticework of living, dead,
    through which morning-glories,
Skeezix, lift the cartoon from the dead woman's face,
in decomposition she is beginning to stir,
"she" a sound, mommymurmur,
this surf a vast sail in which I am trauma,
    dream, a drama of thrums, loose and fast,
a stripe in the gale, hawser, octopus,
like cream words rise to the top
                of the skyscraper,
the rich peer down, the cream
                        crowds,
to be vertical is to be nasal, I ebb,
    a slaughtered monkey
comes up to me, our fingers in our
        fingers, even at guillotine
the touch of Venus, the kissing beheadeds,
sukra rakta sukra rakta sukra rakta
is the sound of dialectical conjunction,
white semen red menses
                        combine to form
Ariadne's pink thread, can be drawn
                        through stone,
ocelot-spangled morning, I am free,
free and embedded, multiform,
    unformed, unproven . . .

Is this what it feels like to be dead?
Whitman's glove comes off revealing

172

no word is foreign, call me Abner,
go suck a snake,
                    as if between each word
a broken tightrope, the walker slowly
                    curling in space,
maggot boy, bagworm, sending a thread
                    into Hell,
and watch the damned ascend, thread
loaded with Theresa and Flip Phillips,
American quilt, as Sousa passes
                    through, Bach pounds
on his lemonade stand. Fuck you and
        your formal design,
Columbus, I refuse to inherit your meter,
as well as your meter maids. I refuse
        the four-square detritus of
the narrative voyage, I peer down
        off the edge of this world
into the eyes of whoareyouman? into
        his central, single eye,
into his soma, the inkwell through which
                    he draws his weenie.
Let Death dance with the Devil,
    cloak them, give them more rein.
Respect the ways in which puns do not work,
are asocial, refuse to hump, the way
    puns are words acrawl on
each other, dumb to each other,
mute synthesis,
                    nothing penetrates,
all is in isolation, every kink of me,
this brick in isolation with its dirt,
the Halloween "wounded child"
more wounded than you can know.
Refuse and accept, make words per-
    form the Buddha,
out go in come, ant and lout, sound is
    a razor,

respect the beggar's hone, his home
  is navel,
amniotic surf, poorest madre.

     Then Angelica Vasquez
washed her feet and put on tan lady shoes
so as to honor us, the visitors   [Atzompa]
               to her craft,
to her *ofrenda*, fruit softening in
  a corrugated corner,
the poor craftswoman offering us
  a choice of beer,
black mole, delicious rice, her roof
  the sun's drum,
her dirt yard infant traipsed,
I visit her here, one of her near-
               dead,
white spook, obtuse as a Spicer
  baseball,
roll onto my back, dog gesture,
  dog fashion to the sun . . .

Can you tell me if this needs revision,
  Mictlantecuhtli,
or can I inject it directly into your
  veins?
Have I sacrificed something here,
or have I been toweling my behind?
Is this lethal enough for you,
  Lord of the Oaxacan Dead,
or is it still in surgical gloves?
Once the poem is skinned, it
  cannot be recarpeted
no matter the amount of hobnails
  on its sole reader's boots.
"I want to write poetry equivalent   [Peter Redgrove]
  to the insanity of

174

flowers here." Wallow in language's
                    fertile mud,
but be aware: there is a cossack
    between the eyes of every reader,
dancing at the speed of madness and
this cossack does not like to be disturbed
by what you do. Thus antler to
    antler in double
backgrounded gridlock. Poet and
    reader: two males
or two viers for *the world*? Is there
    an outside when
we make contact with the brains of heaven?
Yes, and it's all so much copal,
asunderwritten by the breath of trees,
trees deep in the cemetery of your
        fig and mine, or
my errant lay, I've lost it,
                    shallow in
a phrase going without a some-
            where,   .
how threadbare can you be?
How much emptiness can you plow,
man with a fishy odor,
are these word ruts fertile, he
            worried,
only seconds earlier outside of
    the left brain's
tentacular blow . . .

            This is my studio, my
                    mind,
    this is my harmony in red . . .

        Knot of 3 wailing   [November 2]
    on their knees men, feet

half-sandaled toward us on
side benches, the barren floor
the jarred candles aflicker as if
  nudged by their kinetic
bunching, shadowed, all mouth
and dusty soled, huaraches bending,
          the graveyard sanctuary at Teo-
                          titlan del Valle,
we're here for Arnulfo's dad (he
            calls him),
dead now 1½ years,
                slop of beer drooling
across the grave mound, we drink the
  rest of the small Corona, room-
                temperature,
cempasúchil, network of this ensouling,
clumps of friendly mourners, one
  plot thick with green stalks,
Karen Tortuga has a black ceramic
                turtle center
of her plot,
          Zapotec silk knotted
  twisted braids, blocky small women,
Arnulfo's mother shaking with 1½
      year old agony of loss,
he was there but she couldn't see him   [the Mendoza
force of the invisible dead visible   living room in
  to the heart   Teotitlan del
which tries to grow eyes, pain of heart   Valle]
        blindness. Copal smoke:
  winding, disappearing *forms*?

rest in peace my mother
rest in peace my father
to Oaxaca I have come
as if to bless the life you me gave,
and say it backward to
span 22 years of no grave

176

cempasúchil no copal hardly a
                              thought
at Equinox when Arnulfo might say
your spirits stand open-mouthed
     by my table—

     Señora Mendoza's sorrow
     sent out grappling hooks
the anger that the dead are dead
the frustration that the clumped men
          as if on one iron hinge
cannot resurrect in chant the
          frustrating invisible berating
                         dead,

who are here,
heart inhabited,
and thus this barbwired heart?
Stonehenge of the heart
protected by barbed-wire?

EPILOGUE

When I genitalize my mind, any one or thing is a mine to be explored.

When I imagine my mind, the brain seems seminal, finite, keen on working its mine forever.

To imagine my genitalization is to know my self as a squid jetting by, or as a rock whose E, said to be unreadable, stares, a runic miss.

I used to think that there was only one missing story, in perpetual feedback, the gap between desire and its fulfillment, the stepping beyond, if only for an instant, onto that anvil heated beyond the grave.

In dream, as one ages, the dress rehearsals become more poignant than opening night. Let them continue to be interrupted by revenants passing, from eternity into dreamtime, across the Muladhara Bridge, starved to dance their realizations on the spongy stage.

Last night, I was in Mexico again, in an awesome half cave half cathedral, with an orchestra pit that flushed out stars. The scenery was organic, the baptism of a cockroach utter magic. Spellbound on my knees, my body still part of our sphere, my head peering beyond the encircling stars, I heard a voice command: "Now look back into that trough where god, cod, pod, rod, sod and nod once pullulated. Can you, using these od blocks, construct a cod-like sodpiece for god's nodding, pod-like rod?"

As at a gasoline pump, the scroll of numbers turns.

Suppose at this century's end, only the 3rd and 4th digits turn. We would be dropped back to 1900, on the eve of *The*

Interpretation of Dreams, so as to be as we were, as if nothing but the passing of static time had occurred, as if we could not bear for all the digits to turn, for 2 to face—through the zero tube—infinity.

Indeed, what would it mean for 2 to face infinity?

2 might be living without the tombal influence of god. Then not only would the judgement of god be ended, as Artaud proclaimed in 1948, but his amoral, ventriloquistic umbilicus, rooted in any Bible or Koran without comparison, would be shredded—

a perilous moment, for then 2 would have to become a self-regulatory (homage to Wilhelm Reich) biune, a kind of double-backed crypt containing the history of laughter, all the vulva grigris, all the phallus jujus, in which the saint who pricks condoms is married to the bastard who imagines, the alchemical and perpetual wedding of Teresa and Sade.

The banquet of the ape's head projected through the earth's table center, held by a nuclear band, the skull top severed, entire populations with chop-sticks eager for live brain, could end—

but for maybe a hundred years the living would have to absorb and assimilate what god's rotting corpse has done to the earth, not knowing if the entire system had been made mortal, or if, once the oceans, ground, and air had been washed, a pristine impermanence, on which a dignified human mortality could be based, might be restored.

Facing this awesome roll call, the individual soul might look like doll casing, the slash and burn of dream little more than a reflection of the unlimited, human capacity for destruction. But it is precisely the imagination that must replace the social drama of reaction to god's rotting corpse. The corpse itself must be delineated, must be resolved within the double-backed crypt of 2 facing infinity.

Now Friedrich Schröder-Sonnenstern wants to say a word: "In the precious slime of vision, my mother's dear mouth became a toothed cavity, her flaccid breasts jetting penises. I painted the SS masculine displacement, how men everywhere raise their lower body that they cannot live with, into a woman's upper body reconstructed as a Devil's Island."

Then a man with AIDS lay down upon me. His feet were huge, weighty, his head immense, his waist virtually nothing. Is he what is left of the Whitman man who received a plunged tongue in his barestript heart? How adhesively *and* romantically we must pay attention to beginnings and endings as the wrap-around of 2000 stares.

In imagination, one metaphor tries to grasp its amoebic split-off to hurl it forward into numerology, myth, any cosmic extension, while what it is anchored in, carnal, mute, as if a Covering Prefix, gestures earthward. Thus this flux, this stasis, this Kaaba moving at relativity with my death.

Reading deep into mortality, numbers curl obscurely. What is going on in that large, green, leather boot, its chimney fuming, with little windows and a stoop, in the childhood clearing? And the old lady, this grizzled, dog-headed gal, has she my report card? Is it written in Farsi? Am I all her children, the only and the many, in the aligator tunnel of that boot, "a boot full of brains," the heart goes forth, as if on elastic, to the other who gives it a good squeeze before releasing the sensation of the abyss back into its cavity.

In eternity—into which god's corpse is spilling oil—Rainer Maria Rilke and Francis Bacon are cleaning up our mess. Rilke curved into himself and stayed. Bacon curved into other men and left. Both found a main at the locks of infinity. Between black cracks the numbers shine!

GRATITUDE & ANNOTATION

For over 20 years, Caryl Eshleman has defined the meaning of "reader" and "editor" for me. As a sounding board, she has been invaluable. While it may be occasionally true à la Ginsberg that "first thought [is] best thought," most of the time, in my case, composition is a slow, percolating process, with material passing through certain filters while other filters are being removed. In these attempts to extract the essence of material whose context is always shifting until it "sets," her responses, mingling confirmation and resistance, have helped me see through superficial clarities as well as groundless obscurities. More specifically, she has rewritten passages (while in draft) or changed the direction of certain poems with a deft phrase and has taught me to allow another person to enter my creative space with love and harmony. I have even sometimes relinquished control of the poem to her to see where it would take us. It is a joy to acknowledge her participation, therefore, in book after book.

I am grateful to Wolfgang Giegerich, a generous correspondent for a number of years, for sharing his ideas with me, some of which have worked their way into certain poems. Because most of Giegerich's writing has not yet been translated from the German, I want to mention here his two essays in *Sulfur* magazine (#21 and #28), as well as Robert Avens' introduction to Giegerich's work at large in *Sulfur #20*.

I am also grateful to Gerrit Lansing, Paul Christensen, Herbert Lust, Eliot Weinberger, Peter Redgrove, and Keith Tuma, who have read and commented on early drafts of *Under World Arrest*. Most of these people will hardly recognize the book in its present form, but they should know that its evolution over the years—from 1989 to 1992 threshed by my translation of César Vallejo's *Trilce*—has been stimulated by their responses.

*

"The Bashō Thrill of Setting Forth": Haibun #1, in the Corman/Kamaike translation of Bashō's *Back Roads to Far Towns*.

"Still-life, with Huidobro": "organiz'd innocence": marginalia to William Blake's *The Four Zoas*: "*Unorganiz'd Innocence: An Impossibility.* / Innocence dwells with Wisdom, never with Ignorance." The Huidobro line is from his poem, "Arte Poética."

"Outtakes": the words "synthesis" and "mêlée" are, in this context, taken from Theodore Enslin and Robert Duncan respectively, who tend to emphasize one over the other as goals for poetry. I see the two forces as co-penetrational.

"Amphimixis": in "Artaud le mômo" (*Oeuvres complètes*, Vol. XII), Artaud states that he was devastated by god, who sought to "sack the ingestion / of his lines," "on the curvature of that bone / located between anus and sex." Such is the location of the lowest, or Muladhara, Chakra ("wheel"), in Tantra subtle body doctrine (see Note on "Navel of the Moon"). Artaud's curved bone evokes both the rim of the Chakra and a bridge, whose two ends might be said to lead to sex and anus, or to fecundity and fecality (and basically, to life and death).

In addressing what he calls "anal and urethral innervations" in his astonishing work, *Thalassa*, Sandor Ferenczi redefines "amphimixis" psychoanalytically as a "synthesis of two or more eroticisms in a higher unity." By a "higher unity," Ferenczi has in mind normal ejaculation, probably what Wilhelm Reich calls "orgasm." Given the subtle and physical body evidence for a full body participation in creative activity, I would extend Ferenczi's "synthesis" to an interplay between sexual and creative realizations. I also draw on his use of "amphimixis"

184

in discussing the "shaft" scene from Lascaux in "Seeds of Narrative in Paleolithic Art" (*Antiphonal Swing*).

"Indiana in the Night Sky": as an immortal to the infant self, mother appears to be the fount of imagination. In my experience, imagination does not clear itself of observational restraints until the image of the body of the mother is totally accessible. By "body" here I include the "huge rock" that Kumarbi fucks in "The Song of Ullikummi," as well as the "Mountain" penetrated by the Algonquin woman (Charles Olson, *The Maximus Poems* IV, V, VI). The latter story-poem is especially striking, for it indicates that women as well as men are to "walk right through the rock of the mountain."

It is said that Caesar was told that his dream of incest meant that he was to conquer the world. For the poet, I would revise this meaning to: fulfillment of psychic incest can enable him or her to invent a world (see "Still-life, with Huidobro").

The real goal, then, is not psychic incest, but poetic parthenogenesis. Poets seek to participate in this power, and I think they must go through mother to get there. Mother, in this sense, is pylon, and it is necessary to pass through her complex ramifications into a vision of oneself as finally separate.

The italicized lines in the poem first appeared as the epigraph to *Indiana*.

"Double Pelican": here is an image of the alchemical "double pelican" (from the cover of John Trinick's *The Fire-Tried Stone*), which, in the way that it is drawn, suggests a sexual reading of the "circulatio."

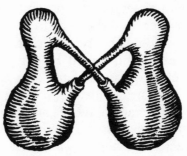

"After Pindar": the article on Sarajevo in *The New York Times Magazine*, July 26, 1992.

"So Be It": the following paragraph from N. O. Brown's *Love's Body* (p. 249) is not only pertinent to this poem, but epigraphic to my poetry at large:

> Knowledge is carnal knowledge. A subterranean passage between mind and body underlies all analogy; no word is metaphysical without its first being physical; and the body that is the measure of all things is sexual. All metaphors are sexual; a penis in every convex object and a vagina in every concave one.

"Strata": Elaine Morgan, *The Descent of Woman*.

"A Cross Section of the Incarnation": Richard Rhodes, *The Making of the Atomic Bomb*, p. 670.

"Venusberg": the headless embracing bisons, part of a spear thrower, comes from Les Trois Frères cave in the French Hautes-Pyrénées. The quotation with which the poem ends is from Tannhäuser (and is contextualized, relative to the deep past, by Hans Peter Duerr in *Dreamtime*).

"Thalassa Variations": writing on Henry Miller in *Genius and Lust*, Norman Mailer proposes that "Miller saw that Lawrence had come to grips with the poetry of sex but none of the sewer gas. Miller would light matches to the sewer gas like nobody who ever lived, and he set off literary explosions, but he never exploded himself over the other side of the divide. He could be poetic about anything and everything except fucking with love." In the poem "This I Call Holding You" (*What She Means*, 1978), I engaged some of my own sewer gas, as well as the world's, as it seemed to invade "fucking with love." Such gas does not magically vanish in the caress. Yet that poem has always seemed inadequate to me, I think now because it is so outwardly directed. Perhaps it was a first step in taking on

186

what might be called the interiority of the sexual embrace.

Over the years I have pondered Sandor Ferenczi's *Thalassa: A Theory of Genitality*, and wondered how his unique argument might shed light on the origin of image making. It occurred to me one evening that being "exploded . . . over the other side of the divide" might involve more than what Mailer implies, i.e., fucking vs. fucking with love. Might not the passage to the other side involve the transformation of sexual release into imaginative work? My experience has been that sexual release charges the mind with fantasy material which subsequently seeks its own release in writing poetry, and that there is something basically frustrating about sexual expression without this subsequent activity.

Ferenczi's argument describes what might lie at the basis of such a frustration. In brief: he proposes that the whole of life is determined by a tendency to return to the womb. Equating the process of birth with the transition of animal life from water to land, he links coitus to what he calls a "thalassal regression": "the longing for sea-life from which man emerged in primeval times." He explains what he means by an "attempt to return to the mother's womb"—and thus to the oceanic womb of life itself—in the following way:

> If we now survey the evolution of sexuality from the thumb-sucking of the infant through the self-love of genital onanism to the heterosexual act of coitus, and keep in mind the complicated identifications of the ego with the penis and with the sexual secretion, we arrive at the conclusion that the purpose of this whole evolution, therefore the purpose likewise of the sex act, can be none other than an attempt at the beginning clumsy and fumbling, then more consciously purposive, and finally in part successful—to return to the mother's womb, where there is no such painful disharmony between ego and environment as characterizes existence in the external world. The sex act achieves this transitory regression in a threefold manner: the whole organism attains this goal by purely hallucinatory means, somewhat as in sleep; the penis, with which the

organism as a whole has identified itself, attains it partially or symbolically; while only the sexual secretion possesses the prerogative, as representative of the ego and its narcissistic double, the genital, of attaining *in reality* to the womb of the mother.

While Ferenczi comments elsewhere on the development of genital sexuality in the female as well as the male, his argument is essentially from a masculine viewpoint, and in this respect ultimately inadequate. However, since it seems to genuinely break new ground from that masculine viewpoint, I will make use of it in what follows, with the above reservation. In one respect, my poem is a compression of, and variation upon, Ferenczi's argument.

To my knowledge, N. O. Brown is the only writer to have heretofore assimilated Ferenczi's theory of genitality into a larger dimension including creativity. In *Love's Body*, Brown even acknowledges the Upper Paleolithic caves as the places in which history begins. Like Ferenczi, Brown is a Freudian, and while he views the Paleolithic caves as the first labyrinths, he fails to reflect on what seems to be their most distinctive characteristic: they are not merely wandering places, or even dancing enclosures, but the sites for the earliest image making. Following Ferenczi, Brown views genitality as ultimately ungratifying, in effect a trap. Ferenczi's proposal that we desire to return to the womb and obviously cannot, in Brown's terms becomes the limitation he calls "genital organization."

Since Brown also draws upon William Blake's vision of the four mental states potentially operative in humanity, it may be useful to point out that from a Blakean viewpoint, to be confined to "genital organization" is to be arrested at the third level of mental expansion (see the poem, "The Crystal Cabinet"), or to be in the State of Beulah. In other words, Blake appears to mean that those who settle for sexual gratification alone are not fully human. For Blake, there is a fourth state, the State of Eden, in which imagination is engaged and realized, and in which that art which we might call great is created. Blake's image for this state is fire in love with fire (from which Yeats undoubtedly got his image of creative unity: the dancer as unidentifiable apart from the dance). While there may be a temporary "gratification of desire" between two people in the State of Beulah, in the State of Eden the other vanishes, and for the individual to avoid plunging into the lowest state—the State of Ulro in which one is simply, unimaginatively, stuck with oneself—one must practice a sort of imaginative androgyny called art. While Brown does not appear to include cave art in his discussion of the labyrinth, I should point out that he ultimately views coitus as a fallen metaphor for poetry.

Were Blake alive today, I am confident that he would make the connection I am about to make: the womb that cannot be returned to à la Ferenczi is imaginatively re-entered when Cro-Magnon crawled into a cave and drew, painted, or sculpted an image. I conjecture that one stimulation for this going into the cave was orgasm itself, which flooded the mind with fantasy material that demanded a fulfillment beyond mundane concerns. Image making, then, can be seen as the attempt to unblock the paradoxical male impasse of genital expression, or, in my poem, it is what the belling deer image "says" to its Cro-Magnon maker, on his back, in that cul-de-sac in Le Portel: "Image is / the imprint of uncontainable omega, / life's twin." In the same stanza, I attempted to draw upon the Freudian/Ferenczian theory of the sexual stages of development, working with the possibility that from childhood on, oral, anal, and genital formations are incorporated in image making, which for the mature individual becomes a kind of fourth dimension (or State à la Blake) that includes the earlier three and pushes beyond.

"Image" sounds "imago," zoologically "an insect in its final adult, sexually mature, usually winged state." It is on this basis that the conjunction of wall, image, and artist is envisioned as a "butterfly" in "The Chaos of the Wise" which follows "Thalassa Variations."

"Homuncula": in 1974, Marjorie Perloff published a long review in *Contemporary Poetry* magazine, called "The Corn-Porn Lyric: Poetry 1972-73," in which the books of 20 poets were put down as being corny *and* pornographic. Set against works by, for example, Ai, Creeley, myself, Jong, Levertov, and Wakoski, were some gloomy lines of Wieners and Rich. Perloff argued that the corn-porn culprits "are those who want to have their cake and eat it too; they wish to be completely uninhibited about sex and yet to respect such time-honored values as fatherhood, motherhood, a 'good' marriage, friendship, fidelity, trust, integrity, or devotion to the sick and the poor." Unlike Wieners and Rich (and the Rimbaud of "Poets Seven Years Old"), we lacked "a sense of extremity, of dangerous desire and demonic possession."

I said what I had to say about all of this in a long response printed in CL in 1975, and only bring the matter up again because my anger at Perloff's flatironing 20 of us into a cliché led me to ponder a poetry that would be both demonic and pornographic. To my mind, Perloff didn't offer any convincing examples in her review (she could have cited Artaud), but her core issue became important for me to deal with. In 1973, I had written a set of poems "by" a Russian dwarf whom I made up named Metro Vavin ("The 9 Poems of Metro Vavin," The Gull Wall). How about a work "by" a woman whose mode of expression involved both horror and pornography? It was Caryl Eshleman who suggested that such a figure might be called Horrah Pornoff. So I made an attempt—and got nowhere. But I did become fascinated, and then obsessed, with creating a feminine persona ("a woman of some sort out of his imagination to prove himself," as Williams put it in A Dream of Love), someone who, unlike Yeats's "Crazy Jane," was not based on a real-life figure, and who would thus be free to be and not to be.

I decided that Horrah Pornoff's manuscript should consist of 77 poems (the number in Vallejo's Trilce), and over the next year completed a fifth draft of the present poem (which in subsequent reworkings became much shorter). I also became interested in how certain editors and friends would respond to "Homuncula," so I took out a PO Box, as Horrah Pornoff, in the local post office, and began to send poems around. Horrah appeared in Charlie Shively's Fag Rag, Bill Mohr's Momentum, and she was featured by Cid Corman in the 4th series of origin (Cid wrote Horrah that at last LA had a poet!). Soon, going

190

to the post office for her mail, and staying involved with her several correspondences (two of which had her fending off people who wanted to date her), grew stale, and I ended the game, which also meant putting aside the manuscript.

In 1990, after reading Camille Paglia's *Sexual Personae*, I went back to the manuscript. Paglia's book made me realize anew the extent to which writers are persona-infested. Not only do we take on "masks" that float forth ghost-like through our personalities, but we are fascinated by expressing what we are not as an aspect of what we are—with the underlying alchemical insight that wholeness consists of a circulation of negative as well as affirmative formations. At that time, I began to see that although Horrah was make-believe, she was also a serious working of persona. Even more, she was an expression of the extent to which the feminine aspects of my personality had fought over the years for their rightful place in my work. She was my inner "little woman," or "homuncula," whom I had become aware of through poetry itself, and her "birth," as it were, was precious for me to work through. I also want to acknowledge that without Marjorie Perloff's review, Horrah Pornoff, as such, would undoubtedly not exist.

"Saddam should feed his people": the title is an overheard remark from an NPR broadcast. The unidentified quotes are from, in order: Noam Chomsky, US Air Force Commander Dick White, The House of Tyrol (a direct mail Georgia retailer), and James McDermott (a physician, before the House Select Committee on Hunger).

"Some Fugal Lubrication": Väinamöinen, who kills the bear Otso, is the magic singer of the Finnish epic, the *Kalevala*.

"Humbaba": in A. David Napier's *Masks, Transformation, and Paradox*, p. 112, there is a depiction of Gilgamesh's antagonist (who Napier considers to be the source of the Greek gorgon). In *Hamlet's Mill*, de Santillana and von Dechend write that Humbaba "appears to correspond to the Elamitic god Humba or Humban, who shares the title 'the prevalent, the strong' with the planets Mercury and Jupiter, and with Procyon (alpha Canis Minoris)." I.e., Humbaba was a Neolithic star.

"Inn of Somewhere": to my knowledge, the too-little-known saxophonist Warne Marsh did not record a version of Charlie Parker's "Koko" (based on "Cherokee" changes). I heard several of Marsh's breathtaking "Koko" solos when he played with Supersax at Donte's in North Hollywood in the 1970s. Among the Marsh records I listen most to are: *Warne Out* (Interplay Records), *Ne Plus Ultra* (Revelation), *The Art of Improvising* (Revelation), and *How Deep, How High* (Discovery). Clark Coolidge wrote me that Marsh dropped dead in Donte's while playing "Out of Nowhere."

"At the Hinge of Creation": the Olson is from *Maximus IV, V, VI*; the De Vries quote is from H. R. Ellis Davidson's *Gods and Myths of the Viking Age*.

"At Labastide": Labastide is a Magdalenian-decorated cave in the French Hautes-Pyrénées, whose sigil is yet to be grasped.

"The Horizon that Doesn't Go Away": after a reading at the Galerie Pierre, in Paris, Artaud noted:

> This reading took place this evening, Friday 18 July 1947, and at moments it was though *I skimmed the opening* of my heart's tone.
> I would have had to *shit* blood through my navel to arrive at what I want.
> For example, three-quarters of an hour's beating with a poker on the same spot . . .
>
> —*Antonin Artaud: Blows and Bombs*, Stephen Barber

"Out of the Kat Godeu": the italicized lines are my translation from a French translation of the Welsh "Kat Godeu." Also known as "The Book of Taliesin"—since it is attributed to a

6th century bard by that name—and "The Battle of the Trees," it is mainly known to English readers in D. W. Nash's Victorian version published in Robert Graves' *The White Goddess*. The French version, translated by Goulven Pennaod, Alain Le Berre, and Guy Etienne, appeared in *poésie bretagne* #8, 1987.

"On Sunlit Garage Front": La Roche-de-Lalinde is a late Magdalenian rock shelter in the French Dordogne. Photos of the "female outlines" may be found in S. Giedion's *The Eternal Present: The Beginnings of Art*.

"Guyton Place": in the late 1980s, the painter/sculptor Tyree Guyton and his wife, Karen, created a unique, ongoing, art installation in a run-down Detroit neighborhood, called "The Heidelberg Project" (after the street on which Guyton's grandfather lived, which was also the central street in the project). Basically, it involved attaching junk and abandoned objects to several abandoned houses and turning them into outdoor sculpture. The street itself, trees, fire hydrants, etc., were also painted and decorated.

The City of Detroit at first welcomed the project, listing it as a must-see for tourists (thus at the height of its popularity, Mercedes and stretch-limos could be seen slowly driving by). After numerous complaints by uncomprehending citizens (who thought Guyton was into Voodoo), the City decided that "The Heidelberg Project" was a public nuisance, and, while leaving scores of crack houses in the same area alone, bulldozed all of the Guyton houses in two stages (1989 and 1991). Not owning the houses, the Guytons simply had no way to protect them.

The poem is a result of several visits I made to the project at which time I made lists of the things attached. There are photographs of the houses in *Sulfur #25*.

"Navel of the Moon": in *Muelos: A Stone Age Superstition about Sexuality*, Weston La Barre offers a well-documented argument that from deep antiquity—even as part of a Paleolithic Ur-Kultur—there has been a worldwide belief that there is a physical connection, via the cerebrospinal canal, between the male brain and semen. On p. 131, he sums up the superstition as follows:

The complex of ideas includes the following: bones are given by the male parent, and bones can magically reconstitute the whole animal. As the main storehouse of bone marrow (muelos), the brain is the source of semen, via the spinal cord. The supply is limited. The fertility of the head is associated to cosmic fertility of the sun, rain, lightning. Fire, light, lightning, and seed are all aspects of the same holy male mystery. The fertility of humans, wild animals, and fields can be increased by collecting severed human heads. Fat-marrow and bones are appropriate sacrifices to the immortal spirits, the eternal gods. Immortality also consists in the "continence" of muelos-seed, achieved in various ways. Adult manhood is not the result of endogenous forces but must be obtained from outside through a variety of methods, including homosexual acts. Virility is secreted with the semen, in all ejaculation of any kind; virility can thus on occasion be made a gift. Loss of manhood, power, and ultimately life itself results from the "spending" of the life-force, which is a finite capital.

While La Barre is undoubtedly medically correct, i.e., that the brain is not the source of semen, the extent to which this superstition is tied into religion, philosophy, sexuality, and war, indicates that it may be at the base of man's attempt to reconcile spirit and matter (or subject and object, or as ancient Hinduism puts it, "I" and "That"). The belief that there is a connection between brain and genitals underlies the subtle body doctrine of Tantra (behind which is probably an earlier identification between the ageless serpent and the Great Goddess herself). Tantra proposes that a kind of two-way traffic is possible in the spinal column. The downward energy is inducted via an invisible opening situated in the crown of the skull (probably the fontanel). The upward movement is initiated when a subtle female snake, Kundalini, coiled between anus and sex, is aroused to straighten up and ascend the subtle channel of the spinal column, passing through a series of mandala-discs,

194

called Chakras, on her way to the Ajna Chakra, located between the eyes, as a "third eye." Here, formless contemplation is said to take place, as the initiate achieves a union of the two absolute principles into the unitary Brahman.

In the 1930s, as part of his evolving "function of the orgasm" theory and practice, Wilhelm Reich, with apparently no knowledge of Tantra, sketched out a segmental structure of what he called "character armor." Given his goal of reestablishing plasmatic currents in the pelvis, he began his dissolution of this armor in the regions farthest away from the pelvis. His segments bear a striking resemblance to the Tantrik Chakras:

Reich's "segments"	Tantrik Chakras
ocular ring	Ajna Chakra
oral ring	
deep neck musculature	Vishuddha Chakra
chest ring	Anahata Chakra
diaphragm & solar plexus	
large abdominal muscles	Manipura Chakra
pelvis	Svadhishthana &
	Muladhara Chakras

More recently, in his *Typhonian Trilogy*, the Aleister Crowley scholar, Kenneth Grant, has linked the Qabalistic Tree of Life, astrology, and Tarot, with the Tantra subtle body, in an esoteric web of sexual ritual relating to the Vama Marg, or Left Hand Path, which in itself is tied not only into worship of the Primal Goddess but into making contact with extraterrestrial entities. Curiously, while Grant occasionally quotes Reich, and seems to be familiar with his work at large, he does not mention Reich's ideas about segmental armoring.

As one who has not practiced any form of Tantrik ritual, my experience in these matters is limited to the following: while in Reichian therapy in the late 1960s, I experienced an eruption up my spine that is described in the Introduction to my book *Fracture*. Secondly, since the early 1970s, I have been aware of a phenomenon I call "antiphonal swing." Orgasm has often been followed by a period of relaxation that is fantasy-intensive (identified in some Tantrik sects as *maithuna*), and occasionally hallucinogenic. The images that occur point toward a renewal of creative work, which in its own way leads to a renewal of sexual desire. It seems antiphonal because the imagination and the genitals function like the far swing points of a pendulum, involved with each other's momentum.

Two final points in this regard: one of the earliest appearances of oracular display that I am aware of, initially from Africa, and more recently documented in Haiti, is the figure of a snake priestess straddling a box containing a snake. Penetrated by the "god," she writhes as the oracle speaks from her mouth. Might the Tantra Kundalini system represent an evolution of an earlier system in which an actual snake was used?

In *The Magic Revival*, Grant writes: "The incubus or succubus is the exteriorization, or extrusion, of the satyr in each individual. It represents the subliminal Will; in effect, the Dwarf Self or Holy Guardian Angel. It is this principle in man that is immortal, and it is inextricably bound up with sexuality, which, in turn, is the key to its nature and the means of its incarnation." In a subsequent chapter, Grant writes that "after intimate and persistent intercourse with the Angel has been established, He utters the Word."

Both the snake priestess and the Holy Guardian Angel involve what for poets has been variously called Angel, Muse, or in Lorca's remarkable essay, the Duende, and it now seems to me that the three are facets of a single figure. It may be that the snake priestess enacts the oldest appearance of this figure, and that Aleister Crowley, in contact with Aiwass and other extraterrestrials, was performing a 20th century variation on this grand and mysterious theme. It would seem possible that in the spinal traffic through Chakras and segmental rings is encoded that force which drives us into another's arms and occasionally sings through us when we write. As we approach the millennium, the poetics of these formations cry out for revelation.

Both Aztec and Greek mythologies associate the birth of inspiration with an animal and a warrior god. As Coatlicue is beheaded the two rattlesnakes that rise from the sacrificial urn her body has become are accompanied by Huitzilopochtli, the god of war. And as Medusa is decapitated, not only does winged Pegasus spring forth, but he is accompanied by the warrior Chrysaor. In both cases, the "uprisings" made possible by earlier pregnancies evoke not only Kundalini flashing up her spinal channel, but also sacrificial killing as *the* primordial soul-making. While we do not sacrifice bulls to Zeus today, who is to say that the creative mind does not suffer My Lai and El Mozote? The myths tell us that inspiration is inextricably bound to sacrifice and war, and that its release involves our genitals, guts, hearts, and brains. I tremble in attempting to gauge the distance, if there is one at all, between Perseus's falchion and a Salvadoran Army machete. I also find it compelling that unlike the Greeks who allow inspiration the detachment of an escaping winged horse, the Aztec image locks the twin "serpent power" to the place of mayhem. To me, this suggests that poetic inspiration is not to divorce itself from the sacrificial landscape that offered it a soul. It is this disturbing sense of a simultaneous adhesion to, and imagining of, the real that I have tried to bring home in this book.

[Ypsilanti,
December, 1993]

Printed June 1994 in Santa Barbara & Ann
Arbor for the Black Sparrow Press by Mackintosh
Typography & Edwards Brothers Inc. Text set in
Goudy by Words Worth. Design by Barbara Martin.
This edition is published in paper wrappers;
there are 200 hardcover trade copies;
100 copies have been numbered & signed
by the author; & 26 lettered copies have been
handbound in boards by Earle Gray each with a
holograph poem/drawing by Clayton Eshleman.

Photo: Nina Subin

Under World Arrest is the eleventh collection of poetry by Clayton Eshleman to be published by Black Sparrow Press. Eshleman is also the translator/co-translator of César Vallejo, Aimé Césaire, Antonin Artaud, Michel Deguy, Vladimir Holan, and Bernard Bador. Between 1967 and 1973, he edited twenty issues of *Caterpillar* magazine; in 1981, he founded *Sulfur* magazine, currently in its 34th issue, and based at Eastern Michigan University where Eshleman is a Professor in the English Department. He is also the recipient of the National Book Award, a Guggenheim Fellowship in Poetry, and several fellowships in poetry and translation from the National Endowment for the Arts and the National Endowment for the Humanities. Paul Christensen's study of Eshleman's poetry, *Minding the Underworld: Clayton Eshleman and Late Postmodernism*, was published by Black Sparrow Press in 1991.